The English Reformation to 1558

T. M. PARKER

The English Reformation to 1558

Second Edition

OXFORD UNIVERSITY PRESS
London   Oxford   New York

First edition published in the Home University Library, 1950
Second edition published as an Oxford University Press paperback, 1966

This reprint, 1973

Printed in the United States of America

Preface to First Edition

TO ATTEMPT, in a book of this size, to do more than draw attention to some of the salient features of the first epoch of the English Reformation, would be an impossibility. I have done no more, therefore, than to trace the general outlines of the story with the idea of assessing, so far as can be done, some of the chief forces which moulded the Reformation in this country, both in its resemblances (closer than are sometimes admitted) to the Continental Reformation, and in its differences from that movement, of which both the insular position of England and the peculiar character of English society, as it had evolved in the Middle Ages, were the causes. If I can induce some readers to make a closer study of a fascinating period in English history, I shall be satisfied.

Throughout I have tried to set the theological controversies of the age in closest relation to the secular political tendencies of the sixteenth century. In my judgement neither can be understood without the other, and most erroneous understandings of events result from failure to treat both together. This may perhaps enhance the topical usefulness of the book to modern readers; for England of to-day cannot be understood without some knowledge of this, one of the most formative periods in her past. If it be true, as I believe it is, that England is one of the few countries in which the conflict of the Reformation and the Counter-Reformation has never yet been fought to a finish, then the key to many tensions of the present day lies partly in the events here described.

My grateful thanks are due to my colleague, the Rev.
F. J. M. Dean, who has read the proofs of this book for
me and compiled the index.

Oxford, 5 December 1949   T.M.P.

Preface to Second Edition

THE RE-ISSUE OF THIS BOOK in a new format has enabled
me to incorporate recent knowledge and to modify phrases
which had seemed to me in some respects inaccurate or mis-
leading. In particular, the text has been corrected, I trust satisfactorily, in the light of the conclusive research of Dr. J. Scarisbrick upon the charge brought against the whole body of the
clergy in 1531 (p. 47), and the work of Sir John Neale, con-
solidated in the first volume of his *Elizabeth I and her Parliaments*, which demonstrates that the otherwise mysterious Protestant opposition to the Supremacy bill in the Commons was
tactical, designed to hold up legislation until the Queen agreed
to immediate restoration of the Second Edwardine Prayer Book,
not based, as has been suggested, upon Calvinist dislike of royal
supremacy as such. Dr. G. R. Elton and Professor A. G.
Dickens's important studies upon Thomas Cromwell, whilst
they make me feel that I may at some points have been less
than just to that enigmatic figure, still do not influence me to
think that I have fundamentally misinterpreted his character
and aims. The bibliography has once more been revised and
new books recommended. As it now stands I hope that this
little book presents a reasonably correct outline, as objective
as may be, of our present state of knowledge about the pre-
Elizabethan English Reformation. It is my hope in a companion
volume to continue the story from 1588 to the Revolution of
1688, which seems to me to mark the end of the acute period
of religious reorientation and dispute in this country and to
usher in an era in which religious issues to a great extent changed
their character.

Oxford, 3 April 1966   T.M.P.

Contents

1

Church and State in Medieval England

THE RELIGIOUS ORGANIZATION OF ENGLAND down to the sixteenth century followed the pattern common to all Western Europe at the time. The West had accepted the Christian faith as taught by the missionaries who evangelized that half of the Mediterranean basin, the countries of the Atlantic seaboard and Central Europe up to the Pripet Marshes. In doctrine therefore the Christians of this area recognized as the orthodox Catholic Faith the type of Christianity defined by the great ecclesiastical councils of all Christendom from the fourth century onwards and further developed by the Western Church after the schism of East and West in the early Middle Ages. Arianism, an alternative explanation of the Christian revelation, had indeed been brought into the West by the Teutonic barbarian invaders of the fifth century, but by the eighth century that was dead and thereafter there was no cleavage on major issues of faith in the Western world, although throughout the Middle Ages heretical groups without much cohesion tried to spread their views and were in consequence persecuted by the authorities of Church and State. With this exception religion was uniform all over the West and the ultimate bond of union between the different nations in ecclesiastical matters was a common acknowledgement of the traditional authority of the See of Rome, whose supremacy was unchallenged.

With this doctrinal unity and common recognition of Roman hegemony there had grown up a substantial uniformity of worship and everyday religious practice, which meant that, despite many differences of custom in detail, the traveller who visited the many different countries of the West would have felt at home in any church he chose for worship and able to recognize its services as those with which he had been familiar from childhood, whilst the devotional practices and outlook of the people would have seemed to him closely akin to the ideas of his own countrymen. In organization too the ecclesiastical system varied little from place to place. The smallest unit was the parish with its church; churches were linked with one another in dioceses (of very varying size) and groups of dioceses formed provinces, each under the presidency of an archbishop, the whole finding its ultimate centre of life and authority in the Papal Curia. A uniform system of church law, assembled in the bulky *Corpus Juris Canonici*, determined the juridical relations of all grades of the clergy and laity in ecclesiastical matters, and was administered and enforced by a hierarchy of ecclesiastical courts once again centering in Rome. At first sight at least Western Christendom on its ecclesiastical side presented an impressive spectacle of unity and uniformity on a scale never attained since. Further we may add to our picture the fact of a theology, developed and taught in the universities, which, however fertile in evolving questions for dispute, could yet assume the common acceptance both of broad principles of doctrinal authority—the binding nature of the conciliar definitions of the Church, the inspiration and truth of Scripture, and the reverence due to the thought of the Church Fathers of earlier centuries—and of a uniform dialectical method of approach to Christian thought. Studied in close relationship to a philosophy which, even if much more diverse than used once to be thought, started from basic assumptions common to all civilized thought, this theological tradition involved a unity of Christian thought which was very real.

For many reasons this unity of the Western Church was in decay in the fifteenth century; the forces which were ultimately to dissolve it can be traced back at least to the century before. Yet the decay was not yet fully apparent, whatever symptoms were presented to those who had eyes to see by such episodes as the Great Schism of the Papacy (1378–1418), the Wycliffite movement in England and the Hussite in Bohemia, or the quarrels between Popes and Councils of the fifteenth century, not to speak of less dramatic signs of growing tension and disunity. But the framework remained as it had grown up in the period of the later Dark Ages and the Middle Ages proper. In particular the relations between the religious and the secular organization of human life to which it had given birth, not without great struggle and dispute, were as they had now been since the work of the Hildebrandine Reform in the late eleventh and early twelfth centuries.

These relations are not easy to understand in a Europe now for four centuries accustomed to the idea of unitary sovereignty. Whether rightly or wrongly most men now take it for granted that there can be in any country not more than one supreme power, that which we term the sovereign State. All coercive authority is assumed to reside ultimately in the hands of the State (whether that State be constituted by popular choice or not), and only by the State's delegation can any body of citizens impose their will upon others. Associations other than the State itself and those empowered by it are purely voluntary bodies whose power only to discipline their members rests upon the consent of those members themselves and whose only final means of self-preservation is expulsion. Religious bodies fall into this last category and, even where the State has not yet become wholly neutral in matters of religion, it is only by permission of the secular power that national churches exercise authority upon their members.

The medieval idea of things was far otherwise. Even in purely political matters the conception of undivided sovereignty was in its infancy; when one came to consider the whole sphere of human life it would have been denied by all accepted opinion. There were not one, but two powers which had, by divine decree, rights over the individual. As a citizen he was indeed subject to the *regnum*, the political State which demanded his obedience. But he was also a member of the Church and as such was subject to the priestly power, the *sacerdotium*, instituted by Christ with the duty of ruling and directing towards the attainment of salvation every baptized soul. And the *sacerdotium* was neither the delegate of the *regnum* nor subject to it; indeed an extreme school of thought held that the exact contrary was the case, that kings and emperors were subject to the Pope even in temporal matters and derived their right to rule from God through him. With few exceptions no medieval man denied that in purely spiritual matters the Church's authority came direct from God and was limited by no earthly power. Nor was the Church a voluntary society; to desert it was to commit a crime against the whole order of things established since the Christianization of Europe and therefore a Christian State must if necessary aid the Church to retain in obedience those subject to her by baptism. In so doing the State was not enforcing its own authority; it was lending its monopoly of force to an independent power which had the right to make its own rules and demand the State's help in carrying them into effect.

This meant the existence side by side in every country of two sovereign powers ideally intended to work in partnership and harmony. Men's souls were in the keeping of the Church: men's bodies in that of the State. Therefore in the sphere of legislation the State did not profess to bind the Church except in so far as her members were also members of the State, owing it allegiance and service in temporal matters. The Church herself determined her standards of doctrine and decided what was orthodoxy and what heterodoxy. The Church laid down the Christian moral code and rules of ecclesiastical law. When either of these was violated by rebels the Church enforced them by excommunication or penance, and when these failed to restore obedience called in the physical force of the State. But the doctrine and the rules so imposed were hers, not those of the political power, which had no direct share in framing them and could not alter them.

Moreover the ecclesiastical power was supra-national. As has been said, its ultimate centre was in Rome, where the Pope had come increasingly to be viewed as an absolute ruler whose decisions and judgements bound the whole Church beyond appeal. Local Churches could legislate for themselves only in such matters as were left open to them by gaps in the 'common law' which had been established by Popes or General Councils of the whole Church; provincial or diocesan canons bore the same relationship to the general canon law as do municipal bye-laws to the common and statute law of England to-day. In each land therefore the local Church, which formed a parallel and independent power to that of the political State, was but the representative of a central power by which it was controlled; Western Europe possessed one unified ecclesiastical organization and a series of independent political powers in local relationship to it within their geographical boundaries.

To complete our picture we must note that the medieval Church was emphatically a clerically controlled body. The laity had no voice in doctrinal decisions, in legislation, or in the administration of discipline. Their duties were to take their part (incidentally an increasingly passive part) in the worship of the Church, to make use of her sacraments and other spiritual aids to salvation, and to obey the Church's directive in order to regulate their lives towards the gaining of that eternal life which the Church existed to make available to men. Thus, inasmuch as the clergy were the active and authoritative members of the Church, it was easy to think of them as being in themselves the Church and to make 'Church' and 'clergy' convertible terms. The two powers in every Christian land appeared to be, not so much the community organized on its spiritual side on the one hand and on its secular side on the other, as just simply clergy and laity. Recognition of the fact that the laity were members of the Church and the clergy members of the State could very easily fade into the background.

Such was the general arrangement of Church and State relationships in the Western half of the European Continent

at the beginning of the Reformation period and, as has been
said, England was no exception to the rule. It is essential to
grasp this fact if one is to understand the revolution effected
by the changes of Henry VIII's reign and the way in which
a path was thus opened for a doctrinal and liturgical Reformation which went far beyond anything contemplated when the
first breach with Rome was made. Everywhere in Europe
the Reformation involved the sweeping away of the old
system of Church and State, but it is the peculiarity of England
that here the constitutional revolution came before the adop-
tion of a new religion instead of being accomplished, as
elsewhere, by the very impetus of that new theology itself.
But in either case the starting position is the same: the medieval
polity just sketched.

There were, however, features in the English situation
which differentiated it from what obtained in some other
places and also were to have considerable influence upon the
course of events. One was the prestige and traditional
authority of the English monarchy, which, however shaken by
the political disturbances of the fifteenth century, remained
essentially intact and could be quickly revived and made more
effective than ever by the Tudors. The central power in
England had both retained its authority from Anglo-Saxon
days against the feudal particularism which went so far in
parts of the Continent, and developed earlier than other
monarchies an efficient system of law and government.
In the course of the later Middle Ages it had, without parting
with its very real powers of personal rule, taken into partnership, both in local government and in the central institution known as Parliament, two of the most politically active
and influential classes in the land, the lesser gentry of the
'knight of the shire' class and the richer burgesses of the
towns. Thus the monarchy was in a better position to exercise
a leadership not easily to be shaken than was the case, for
example, in France or Germany or Spain, the only powers
of comparable size. Nor was the nobility, weakened in the
Wars of the Roses, in any position to form an effective aristo-
cratic alternative to popular monarchy. Only the willingness

of most Englishmen to be led, gladly or reluctantly, by a monarchy heavy with tradition and efficiently equipped with organs of government can explain the control which the English central government was able to exercise over events at almost all stages of the Reformation, or the surprising ease with which Henry VIII was able, within less than ten years, to carry through a complete reversal of the previous relations of Church and State. It is probably true to say that only the English monarchy could have carried through the English Reformation without destroying the country: no other contemporary autocracy could have accomplished such a *tour de force*.

It is well, however, to remember that in attempting such a revolution as he made Henry VIII started with some initial advantages which he inherited and did not create. The English Crown in some respects enjoyed a stronger position in relation to the Church even in the Middle Ages than did other monarchies. The Hildebrandine movement for ecclesiastical independence, which created the characteristic polity already described, had a late start in England, partly because of the normal time-lag with which ideas are apt to cross the English Channel, partly because Hildebrand himself, fully occupied by his conflict with the Emperor Henry IV, was content to leave William the Conqueror, of whose loyalty to principles of practical church reform he was assured, to exercise without question in England a considerable control of the Church. William was used in Normandy to the traditional system by which, whilst the ultimate authority of the Holy See was acknowledged, in practice all save the greatest ecclesiastical affairs were settled by the local Church under the close supervision of the Duke. This conception of a *Landeskirche* he continued in England, combining it with the close connexion between monarchy and Church inherited from his Anglo-Saxon predecessors. Thus, although it was to him that the English Church owed the establishment of separate ecclesiastical courts, he maintained a close control over church legislation and administration and prevented for the time being that continual recourse to Rome in the day-to-day working of the ecclesiastical machine which was to become the rule in the later Middle Ages. Though his system broke down in the series of conflicts between Kings and Archbishops of Canterbury which culminated in the murder of Becket in 1170, the tradition remained to the extent that the English monarchy had always a jealous eye on ecclesiastical privilege and, when opportunity offered, was ready to filch back into its hands anything which in the past it had been forced to concede.

Thus, though John was forced in 1213 to recognize the Pope as overlord even in temporal affairs, and to surrender the control of episcopal appointments which from Anglo-Saxon times the monarchy had regarded as part of its pre-rogative, by the time of Edward I one finds the papal suzer-ainty ignored and, by the time of Edward III, even the tribute which symbolized it repudiated. Never again did the theory of papal temporal supremacy find many supporters in England. And, as an outcome of the struggle of the Crown with the fourteenth-century Papacy over the matter of 'provisions'—the papal claim to fill ecclesiastical benefices at will with its own nominees—the Kings of England eventually won back in practice the power of nominating bishops. By the mid-fifteenth century it was the understood practice that, with a certain give and take on both sides, the King nominated to the Pope those whom he wished to occupy English sees. (So much was this the case that Edmund Dudley, writing soon after Henry VIII's accession, could use the royal appoint-ment of bishops as an argument in support of his proposition that the King was the ground out of which the love of God, the root of the *Tree of Commonwealth*, grows.) The conflict over provisions had other results than this. It led not only to the famous Provisors legislation of Edward III, but to the Praemunire statutes designed to prevent the Papacy from using its judicial and administrative powers to defeat, or force the repeal of, the laws which hindered the Pope from providing to English benefices.

It was in fact the 'Great' Statute of Praemunire of 1393 which was to provide the weapon with which Henry VIII began his assault upon the independence of the clergy. Designed to checkmate an attempt of Boniface IX to bring pressure to bear upon the English episcopate to obtain the repeal of the Provisors statutes, this statute was intended at its enactment merely to introduce a temporary 'blind eye to the telescope' policy, by excluding from the realm the documents by which the Pope might inflict censures upon the bishops who were not supporting his move. But, by a process of wide interpretation which has not infrequently marked legal developments in England, it was used in the fifteenth century to interfere with ecclesiastical jurisdiction whenever the government found it convenient to do so and was thus available for the second Tudor to use against Wolsey and subsequently against the whole English clergy.

If one takes into account these and other ways in which the monarchy, without much open conflict but with considerable persistency, clung to all it could of its powers in church matters and stealthily won back some of the ground it had to yield in the heyday of the high medieval doctrine of ecclesiastical independence, one can see that the sixteenth-century changes, startling as they were, were not the mark of quite so great a revulsion of feeling as we are apt to imagine. From the first days of the civil recognition of Christianity under Constantine, Christian temporal rulers had done their best to secure and retain control of this new and significant force in human affairs, the Christian Church. In the Middle Ages they had been forced to acknowledge in practice, though always with some resentment, the doctrine of the Church as *imperium in imperio*, or rather, *imperium iuxta imperium*. But the notion of undivided civil sovereignty, inherited from the Roman Empire, remained dormant, ready to reassert itself when the State regained strength after the eclipse of centralized power in the Middle Ages, as it did with startling violence as the sixteenth century came into sight. Here again England is no exception to a fairly general rule. But, as already indicated, the English monarchy through historical circumstances already possessed real advantages when the time came for a clash with the medieval theory.

2

Religion in England in the Early Sixteenth Century

THE PICTURE OF THE MEDIEVAL CHURCH as an authoritative sovereign body with coercive rights over its members given in the last chapter may too easily have given the impression of a soulless ecclesiastical machine having very little connexion with religion as such. We shall, however, gain a false idea of medieval religion if we view it solely in this light. Undoubtedly the Church was cumbered with a great deal of administrative red tape, which obscured her *raison d'être* both in the eyes of the ordinary faithful and in those of the officials who worked the creaking engine of church government. The legalist bias, which caused the very nature of the Church to be juridically conceived, is very apparent in the later Middle Ages; the Church was dominated by her canonists and the ordinary layman's contacts with his ecclesiastical superiors were too apt to be coloured by his experience of the Courts Christian. With these he was likely to be involved many times in the course of his life. Not only did he have to report to them when any question arose of wills or of matrimonial matters—two subjects regarded as within the jurisdiction of the Church—but his daily life was subject to the censure of the archdeacon's court, before which he might be brought and put to penance for such public sins as slander, fornication, or neglect of church festivals. The irritation caused by the perpetual intervention of ecclesiastical law into the layman's life, and still more by the arbitrary, expensive, and sometimes corrupt procedure of the church courts, was widespread and could be used, as Thomas Cromwell found in 1532, when he began the attack upon the Church's autonomy by introducing into the House of Commons the *Petition of the Commons against the Ordinaries*, to stir up an agitation for the abolition of the old system. There was not too much exaggeration in the complaints voiced in that document that many of the King's

most humble and obedient subjects, and specially those that be of the poorest sort . . . be daily convented and called before the said spiritual ordinaries, their commissaries and substitutes *ex officio*; sometimes at the pleasure of the said ordinaries and substitutes, for malice without any cause, and sometimes— at the only promotion and accusement of their summoners and apparitors, being very light and indiscreet persons, without any lawful cause of accusation or credible fame proved against them, and without any presentment in the visitation—be inquieted, disturbed, vexed, troubled, and put to excessive and insupportable charges for them to bear, and many times be suspended and ex-communicate for small light causes upon the only certificate of the proctors of the adversaries,

or that in heresy cases the ordinaries or their subordinates

use to put to them such subtle interrogatories, concerning the high mysteries of our faith, as we are able quickly to trap a simple, unlearned, or yet a well-witted layman without learning, and bring them by such sinister introduction soon to his own confusion.

But religious life in England was not confined to canon law and its administration, all too prominent as that side of the Church's activity was. The ordinary Englishman, after all, was more frequently in his parish church than in the arch-deacon's court and it was there that he was most conscious of his membership of the Church. In trying to estimate the state of religious feeling in England when the Reformation began we must consider first the nature and depth of popular worship and devotion. And first of all we must take into account the fact, attested by foreign visitors, that the standard of outward observance was high—higher than in Italy for example. Not only were the Sunday Masses well attended but on weekdays there were many to be found in church. The churches too were used for private prayer—notably the recitation of the Rosary or of the popular Office of our Lady by individuals or groups. The care and adornment of the parish church was the concern of its parishioners, as the evidence of churchwardens' accounts shows, and, according to the author of the *Italian Relation,* 'there is not a parish church in the kingdom so mean, as not to possess crucifixes, candlesticks, censers, patens and cups of silver'. His statement must be set off by visitation evidence of neglect in country churches, but it is probably substantially true, at least of the town parishes. In general the English took an interest in their churches and gave lavishly to them in life and by bequest after death.

All this and much else argues a noteworthy outward zeal for religion. But one may well try to go beneath the surface and inquire how far we are seeing the outward signs of deep inward devotion. Such historical probing of the minds of men is always difficult in the nature of the case. But something may be done by ingenious search for evidence not always considered by historians. One noteworthy attempt of this kind has been made by M. Pierre Janelle in his *L'Angleterre catholique à la veille du schisme* by an investigation of the statistics of religious publications by English printers and continental printers working for the English market in the latter part of the fifteenth and earlier part of the sixteenth century. Though, as he points out, the mere publication of a work is no proof of its being read, evidence of repeated editions of the same work does indicate a demand for it and it is on this assumption that he proceeds. From his investigation of the figures two interesting conclusions can be drawn. One is the high proportion of pious books to the total produced. (For example of seventy-four works issued by Caxton between 1470 and 1490 at least twenty-nine were of this nature; of fifty-four by Wynkyn de Worde between 1491 and 1500 at least thirty fall into this class. In all, of 349 books printed between 1468 and 1530, 176 were religious.) This seems to indicate a demand for religious literature among the relatively small literate English public of the day. But even more interesting is the relative popularity of different kinds of religious books, as shown by the call for reprints. From this it appears that English taste ran especially upon lives of the Saints (usually of a highly legendary nature), sermons (no doubt bought by clergymen who found composition difficult), and books of devotion; both manuals of prayer and books on the spiritual life were also much in demand.

It is this last category which throws most light upon our question. Though many may have been bought and not used, the fact that such works, of which not a few dealt with high levels of spirituality, were in demand would seem to show that there were a good number of people who were trying to practise a more than formal religion. This indication is all the more significant in that such interests do not appear very noticeably in the later part of the century when the turmoil of the Reformation was on; both Catholics and Protestants then seem too deeply immersed in controversial writing and preaching and provocative attendance at the services of their predilection to spare much time for spiritual development; it was not until the seventeenth century that interest in prayer and mysticism revived. But it would seem that England of the epoch just before the breach with Rome was a land in which one could find a good deal of deep religion.

Devotion however was probably not of a very theological or critical type. Janelle calls attention to the neglect of Scripture (evidenced by his book-production figures) as compared with what was happening on the Continent. Whereas in Germany twenty complete translations of the Bible were produced between 1466 and 1522, and in France a thirteenth-century translation was reprinted seven times between 1487 and 1521, all England can show at this period is one solitary edition of the liturgical epistles and gospels in Latin in 1509. Even allowing for those who read Scripture in Latin or French from older manuscripts, this argues a real neglect of the Bible. No doubt Janelle is right in finding an explanation of this in More's contemporary statement, that the stress laid by Lollardy upon Wycliffe's translation had frightened the orthodox from the vernacular Bible. But the conclusion that, to quote Janelle, the reading public 'had no idea of giving themselves an intellectual expression of their religion' seems irresistible when we observe also the paucity of works of technical theology printed at this time. Indeed the same impression would be gained from the obvious theological confusion of the conservative Catholic current of thought in Henry VIII's reign and later. English religion in the early sixteenth century, though often real, was pietistic.

One danger of pietism unaccompanied by accurate religious knowledge is that, at least in the case of those whose piety is demonstrative and superficial, there may be dangerous self-deception, leading to a divorce between religion and morality. That this occurred in England can be shown from many facts. Striking features of the sixteenth century in England are the paucity of really attractive and saintly characters on either side of the Reformation barrier, and the widespread moral corruption. Whether it is the sinister Thomas Cromwell, the timid, intriguing, and *borné* Gardiner, the fanatical Hooper, or the hypothetical John Dudley, avid of money and power, unpleasing characters abound; a Thomas More or a Bernard Gilpin is a rarity. Yet it is by no means the case that all these men were devoid of religious feeling of a sort. They seem in fact to have had a curious ability to combine it with their vices and their cynicism. Henry VIII himself set the fashion. H. A. L. Fisher has said of him that when he 'made a voyage of exploration across that strange ocean, his conscience, he generally returned with an argosy', and it is certain that the King's conscience and his profit had a way of coinciding. His self-righteousness can be amusing, as when, just before his own divorce suit, he described the decree of nullity obtained from Rome by his sister, Margaret of Scotland, as a 'shameless sentence'. He could preach to her too of 'the divine ordinance of inseparable matrimony first instituted in Paradise' and warn her of 'the inevitable damnation threatened against advoutrers'. At the time that he was writing impassioned love letters to Anne

Boleyn, before any authority at all had pronounced upon the validity of his existing marriage, he was 'confessing every day and receiving his Maker at every feast'—the latter a most unusual kind of piety at a time when the laity normally communicated only once a year. When in 1533 he informed Chapuys, the Imperial Ambassador, that God and his conscience were on very good terms, he no doubt meant it quite sincerely; but it is just that consideration that makes one wonder what his conception of personal religion really was. His servants were like him. Cavendish has an unforgettable picture of Thomas Cromwell immediately after the fall of his master Wolsey:

It chanced me upon All-hallown day to come there into the *Great Chamber* at Asher, in the morning, to give mine attendance, where I found Master Cromwell leaning in the great window, with a Primer in his hand, saying of our Lady mattins, which had been since a very strange sight. He prayed not more earnestly than the tears distilled from his eyes.

In the conversation which follows, Cromwell naïvely explains that he is weeping, not for the Cardinal's misfortune, but for his own, and then reveals his plan for leaving the sinking ship. Sixteenth-century England affords a curious study in religiosity divorced from morality, and the reason is probably to be sought partly in the fervent rather than solid piety characteristic of the period just before.

We may conclude, then, that evidence is lacking of any profound dissatisfaction with received religion in the period just before the Reformation. However little they understood it, most men were content with traditional faith and practice. There was however a considerable undercurrent of dissent. It has always been difficult to estimate the significance of the survival of Lollardy from the fourteenth and fifteenth centuries which undoubtedly existed, or to know how many were tinged with it. Spasmodic persecution of heresy went on right up to the time at which Lutheran doctrines began to percolate into England and the martyrs must perforce have been Lollards, as indeed the records of their trials show.

But to arrive at even an approximate estimate of how wide-spread Lollard opinions were is next to impossible in the state of the evidence. Of recent writers, Dr. Maynard Smith considers that 'the proportion of Lollards to the population was much the same as the proportion of Communists to the population to-day'; Dr. Gordon Rupp, on the other hand, without committing himself to figures, is inclined to endorse the martyrologist Foxe's picture of 'the secret multitude of true professors' as an underground movement of considerable extent in these years, and he can quote in his support a statement made during the persecution of the Amersham Lollards in 1506 that Thomas Man, one of their leaders, had with the help of his wife turned six or seven hundred people into heretics. One cannot help thinking that the ecclesiastical affiliations of these two authors to some extent determine their judgements and it is safest merely to say that Lollardy still survived sufficiently to cause periodical uneasiness to the authorities. It must be remembered too that a century and more of persecution had made Wycliffites adept in conceal-ment. As Dr. Rupp puts it, 'For the most part their com-munities moved within the orbit of accepted orthodoxy.' How Lollard propaganda could be spread in such ways may be illustrated from the confession of Robert Hemsted of Steeple Bumstead in the Bishop of London's court in 1518:

Also, he saithe, at Lent last, he was confessid of the sayd Sir Rich. Fox, curat of Bumstede. And when the said Sir Richard had herde this respondentes confession, he axskyd hym, how did he beleve in the Sacrament of thaulter: and then this respondent awnswered, and said as other men doth, That in the blessed Sacrament of thaulter is the very body of Criste. To whom the said Sir Richard said, Nay thou must not do so. For that is not the best way; but beleve thou in the Father, the Son, and the Holy Ghost, and not in the Sacrament of thaulter. And then this respondent said to the forenamyd Sir Richard, I fear ye go about to bryng me in the takyng, that the men of Colchester be in. To whom the said Sir Richard awnswered, What, man, art thou afrayde? Be not aferd. For those serve a better Maister, than ever thou diddest. And so at last, by the motion and techyng of the said Sir Richard; and because he was Prist, this respondent thought, and belevyd that in the blessed Sacrament of thaulter is not the very body of Criste.

When heterodoxy could in this way be taught by a parish priest in the confessional—a fact the more remarkable in that John Tyball, who admitted to having brought Richard Fox to Lollardy, taught the opinion that 'yt was as good for a man to confesse himself alone to God, or els to any other layman, as to a Prieste'—it is difficult to believe that all heretics were detected.

Lollardy in fact was a somewhat amorphous movement by this time, and its followers, who formed their opinions largely by private study of the Scriptures and were not for the most part learned men, held no very definite corpus of doctrine, even changing their opinions, like John Tyball already mentioned, who said that 'abowght a twelve moneth agon he did reason and dispute with Sir Richard Fox, that ther was no *purgatory*; and did hold the same for a season. Howbeit he sayth, he thowght that there was a purgatory ordayned.' In this variableness partly lay the strength of Lollardy. Not only did it suit English individualism, suspicious always of systems, but it enabled the movement to join hands with the much more widespread feeling of anticlericalism, which was hardly articulate enough to be heretical, but was only too ready to take up particular opinions which would annoy the clergy or enable a layman to dispute their authority. The well known episode in 1514 of Richard Hunne, a London merchant tailor, well illustrates this. Hunne had in 1512 lost his case in the ecclesiastical court against a priest who demanded as a mortuary due the sheet in which Hunne's dead baby was carried to the grave. He thereupon cited the priest in the Court of King's Bench, under the Statute of Praemunire. He seems not to have succeeded in this suit either, and meanwhile fell into the hands of the Bishop of London's officials on a charge of heresy, part of the evidence being Lollard books with annotations found in his house. In the bishop's prison he was found hanged, and despite the defence that he had committed suicide, a London coroner's jury accused the episcopal chancellor and two of his servants of murder. The general belief in the city was that Hunne had been 'made a heretic for suing a Praemunire' and done to death in revenge for his original contempt of ecclesiastical jurisdiction. In the course of the public scandal so aroused, Bishop Fitzjames of London begged Wolsey's intervention on behalf of his chancellor on the ground that 'if my Chancellor be tryed by any XII men in London, they be so maliciously set *in favorem heretice pravitatis*, they they will cast and condempne my clerk, though he were as innocent as Abell'. This has been alleged as evidence that the capital was overwhelmingly Lollard, but the evidence does not warrant this. Not only did the city fathers send a deputation to their bishop to remonstrate with him on what they called his 'perillous and haynous wordes', which reflected upon the orthodoxy of the city, but it has been shown that Fitzjames's words have been given a wider scope than they actually had by Hall the chronicler, who substituted 'any clerk' for the '*my* clerk' of the original letter. In any case Fitzjames had a complex upon the subject of heresy, of which he suspected even his orthodox but reforming Dean, John Colet, and in Parliament next year, when a bill was introduced to restore Hunne's property to his children, made the absurd statement, 'I dare not kepe myné owne house for heretiques.' He is not a reliable witness to the sentiments of his see city. What the Hunne case, which provoked repercussions to be discussed later, does show is that there was a deep suspicion and resentment of clerical exactions and jurisdiction, which was easily aroused to fury and would then make the cause of a suspected heretic its own. In many cases this may well have been joined with more or less minor heterodoxies; it is not in itself evidence of a general revolt from Catholicism. Perhaps the matter is best summed up in the words of the *Italian Relation*, which, after testimony to English conventional piety already quoted, goes on to say, 'There are, however, many who have various opinions about religion'—a statement probably true of this country at all times.

Anti-clericalism, springing from dislike of the Church's coercive jurisdiction, its monetary exactions, and the unedifying lives of not a few of the clergy, was indeed the force upon which Henry VIII was chiefly to rely in bringing the clergy into submission to the state. If one asks how the King carried through a policy so generally unpopular as the divorce of Queen Katharine undoubtedly was, by means of a *bouleverse-ment* of the ancient relations of the English Church and State, the only answer can be that the clergy, the chief representatives of the old regime, were not sufficiently popular for laymen to take up their quarrel and that men preferred even royal tyranny to ecclesiastical. The privileges of the Church seemed to many, in the words of a modern writer in a similar context, 'a shabby incubus', and they would not lift a finger to defend them. Nor was there any enthusiasm for the persecution of those who, whether one shared all their opinions or not, had for a century been preaching against the wealth and power of the priesthood. Even so to-day might an old-fashioned Radical feel sympathy with Communists without in the least sharing Marxist opinions.

After about the first decade of Henry VIII's reign, however, dissidence received reinforcement from abroad. In 1517 Luther began his revolt against the Papacy and the medieval system of religion, and Lutheran opinions began to enter England with surprising celerity. They were aided by the considerable English trade with Germany and the Low Countries, which afforded a ready passage to Lutheran writings in the ships which crossed the North Sea—the more so in that the merchant class (as the example of Hunne illustrates) were among those most disposed to criticize the Church. As the least traditional of the nation they were open to new ideas, and it is no doubt true, as many economic historians have claimed, that they were restless under the domination of medieval Catholicism, which looked with suspicion upon trading as an easy occasion of sin, placed the taking of interest upon money under narrow restrictions, and exalted the ascetic life above a career concerned with the wealth of this world. Lutheranism indeed maintained the medieval attitude in the matter of 'usury', but it condemned withdrawal from the world, denied that the clergy were a caste apart from the laity, and denounced the clerical claim to independence of the civil power and to a right of ruling souls. It was fortunate too for the new opinions that their natural route of entry to England brought them first into that lowland half of the country to the south and east which has been throughout English history the home of new ideas, not only because of its geographical propinquity to the outside world, but also because its greater natural wealth (in days before the Industrial Revolution changed the meaning of that term) gave men more time for thought and bound them less to tradition, which always flourishes most where life is hard and experiment dangerous to existence. All through the sixteenth century the strength of Protestantism lay in the south and east, whilst the highland regions of the north and west were the refuge of Catholicism. It is not therefore surprising to find the first evidence of Lutheran propaganda in the south-east.

By 1528 the flood of Lutheran literature was considered enough for Cuthbert Tunstall, Bishop of London, to give the most distinguished lay theologian in his diocese, Thomas More, licence to read Lutheran books in order to write confutations of them in the vulgar tongue—a work which consumed much of his spare time, even during his Chancellorship, from then until 1533. But the literary invasion had begun earlier than this. As early as 1521 Wolsey as Papal Legate circularized the bishops, ordering them to have announcement made in all churches that those in possession of Lutheran books must surrender them to the ordinaries or their officials. And it was at some time during the twenties that the little group of Cambridge dons from whom, more than from any other coterie, English Protestantism found its leaders, began to meet at the White Horse Tavern to discuss the new ideas, whose provenance gained for the inn the sobriquet of 'Little Germany'. The ceremonial burning of Luther's works which followed Wolsey's proclamation may well have been witnessed in Cambridge by William Tyndale, who was destined to be the most effective pamphleteer for Lutheran ideas in English. His withdrawal to the Continent in 1524, after an unsuccessful attempt to persuade Tunstall to let him undertake an English translation of the New Testament, marks an important epoch in the literary campaign. For from his retreat Tyndale, in whom More readily recognized his most dangerous opponent, sent to England not only his translation of the Scriptures, but also a series of vigorous propagandist writings which taught the new faith.

The growing alarm with which the development of this early Protestantism was regarded is shown by the prosecution of heretics during the late twenties. In 1526 there was a trial of certain German Hansa merchants accused of introducing Lutheranism into the Steelyard (the Hansa headquarters in London)—another indication of the routes by which the German Reformation was reaching England. At the same time Friar Barnes of Cambridge was haled before a court for a sermon preached at Cambridge attacking Wolsey's pomp and circumstance and alleged to contain heretical opinions. Next year it was the turn of others of the Cambridge group, including 'little Bilney', most attractive of the early English Protestants. As yet these prosecutions produced no death sentences or martyrs; recantations and imprisonments were the order of the day. Later on the authorities were to prove harsher and the Protestants firmer; Bilney died at the stake in 1531, Barnes with others in 1540. A good deal had happened in the meantime; Henry had broken with the Pope and, after covertly using the Protestants as quasi-allies to suggest to Rome that if his wishes were not granted he might turn Lutheran, he sacrificed them to make a parade of Catholic orthodoxy as a kind of protest against his treatment by the Holy See. We should bear this double-faced policy in mind in considering the great royal proclamation of May 1530 which prohibited Lutheran literature; less than a fortnight before its issue Bishop Nix of Norwich was complaining of the impossibility of suppressing heretical literature in his diocese and relating that many people asserted that the King really favoured it. Indeed, from the time of his quarrel with the Pope, Henry, though never adhering to Protestant doctrine and, on occasion, savagely persecuting Protestants, protected actively or passively some at least of those known to favour the new opinions. But for that fact the religious revolution of Edwards VI's reign would never have succeeded as rapidly as it did.

We must, then, take into account an active, if numerically small, doctrinal opposition to the accepted faith in the years preceding and covering the period of the breach with Rome. It consisted, as we have seen, of two elements, the survivors of English Lollardy and those affected by the incoming gospel of Lutheranism. The former were for the most part simple folk without technical theological education—artisans, peasants, country clergymen, with some merchants and others. They lived upon a simplified Wycliffite tradition which knew little of the more scholastic side of Wycliffe's teaching but inherited his insistence upon Scripture as opposed to tradition and reason, and carried on the criticisms of the earlier Lollards against medieval religious practice, denouncing pilgrimages, the use of images, and similar customs. In some respects they were more radical than the Lutherans: they denied the Real Presence of Christ in the Sacrament, which the latter retained. On the other hand the early Protestant group, whose Mecca was Cambridge, were academic in the highest degree and took up Luther's teachings as *le dernier cri* from abroad; their early hesitations and the development that one can trace in their opinions show this. But, unlike the Lollards, they derived from Germany a more or less systematic theology, centering in the doctrine of justification by faith only, and for that very reason were ultimately to prove a more cohesive and effective revolutionary agency when their time came.

The relations between the two groups are necessarily obscure. There was enough resemblance between their tenets to make it likely that they would regard each other as allies. There seems to be no evidence that the Cambridge group of Reformers had in their early careers been under Lollard influence, but there is, as Dr. Rupp has shown, some indication that the mysterious association of 'Christian Brethren', who appear to have financed some of the early

English Protestant literature and may have been behind Tyndale's translation of the New Testament, was of Lollard origin or at least contained Lollards. An interesting passage in the confession of John Tyball, the Steeple Bumstead Lollard already referred to, who was arraigned for heresy in 1527 (the same year in which the Cambridge Protestants were attacked), shows the kind of relationship there was between the older and the newer religious dissidents:

Furthermore, he saythe, that at Mychaelmasse last past was twelve monethe this respondent and Thomas Hilles came to London to Frear Barons, then being at the Freers Augustines in London, to buy a New Testament in Englishe, as he saythe. And they found the sayd Freer Barons in his chamber; whereas there was a merchant man, reading in a boke, and ii. or iii. more present. And when they came in, the Frear demanded them, from whence they cam. And they said, from Bumstede; and so forth in communication they desyred the sayd Freer Barons, that they myght be aquaynted with hym; because they had herd that he was a good man; and bycause they wold have his cownsel in the New Testament, which they desyred to have of hym. And he saithe, that the sayd Frear Barons did perseve very well, that Thomas Hilles and this respondent were infected with opinions, because they wold have the New Testament. And then farther they shewyed the sayd Frear, that one Sir Richard Fox Curate of Bumstede, by ther means, was wel entred in ther lernyng; and sayd, that they thowghte to gett hym hole in shorte space. Wherfore they desyryd the sayd Frear Barons to make a letter to hym, that he wold continew in that he had begon. Which Frear did promyse so to wryte to hym a letter at afternoone, and to gete them a New Testament. And then after that communication, the sayd Thomas Hilles and this respondent shewyd the Frear Barons of certayne old bookes that they had: as of iiii. Evangelistes, and certayne Epistles of Peter and Poule in Englishe. Which bookes the sayd Frear dyd litle regard, and made a twyte of it, and sayd, A poynt for them, for they be not to be regarded toward the new printed Testament in Englishe. For it is of more cleyner Englishe. And then the sayd Frear Barons delyverid to them the sayd New Testament in Englyshe: for which they payd iii *s.* ii *d.* and desyred them, that they wold kepe yt close. For he wolde be loth that it shold be knowen, as he now remembreth. And after the delyverance of the sayd New Testament to them, the sayd Frear Barons dyd lyken the New Testament in Latyn to a cymball tynkklyng and brasse sowndyng. But what farther exposytion he made uppon it, he cannot tell. And then at afternone they fett the sayd letter of the sayd Frear; whiche he wrote to Sir Richard; and red that openly before them: but he doth not now remember what was in the same. And so departed from hym; and did never since speke with hym, or write to hym, as he saithe.[1]

If, as seems most probable, the 'Frear Barons' of this narrative is to be identified with Robert Barnes, the Cambridge Lutheran, we have here a perfect picture of the meeting of the old dissent and the new. It all rings true: the isolated Lollard hearing in Essex of this unorthodox friar as a 'good man', journeying to make his acquaintance proudly, displaying their hoarded Lollard manuscripts, only to hear that their vernacular scriptures are out of date, and finally going off with Tyndale's Testament, which had just reached England, and a letter from this new influential acquaintance to persuade their parson that in adopting Lollardy he was only keeping abreast of the times. The almost patronizing, if friendly, reception given the two Lollards by Barnes is probably typical of the attitude of those of the 'new learning' towards their less learned predecessors in heresy.

What however of the more articulate opponents of Protestantism and Lollardy? An account of English religion in the early sixteenth century would be incomplete unless one referred to the school of thought represented by More. It is well known that he and others stand apart from the merely conservative and uncritical Catholicism which was the religion of most of the English people, both in their desire for reform on orthodox lines and in the greater depth and reality of their Catholic piety. How far though can the group which originally revolved around Erasmus be considered a party? It would seem, when one considers the matter, that they were a far more loosely knit coterie than has sometimes been realized. What Erasmus, Colet, More, and the others shared in common was a love for Renaissance humanism, combined

[1] Strype, *Ecclesiastical Memorials*. Vol. I, ii (Oxford, 1822), pp. 54-5.

with Christianity. But from the beginning their interpretation of the relationship between these two things varied. Erasmus disliked monasticism; More tried his vocation with the Carthusian monks. With regard to popular devotion to relics Colet displayed, when at Canterbury on pilgrimage, an open impatience which Erasmus, though willing enough to satirize in print the more grotesque forms of contemporary piety, seems to have thought excessive. More revered St. Thomas Aquinas; Erasmus put him with the other scholastics as one who made of theology an over-curious investigation of unprofitable questions. Scholars of this type are the last men to form a party or to agree upon a programme of action. All would have welcomed a practical reform of the more glaring abuses of the contemporary Church, but they were not out to establish a new system. Nor is it true to represent them as reacting into conservatism at the shock of Luther's revolt, as Burke broke with the extremer Whigs under the impact of the French Revolution. The whole trend of Erasmus's view of the Christian life as a progress towards virtue was diametrically opposed to Luther's depreciation of the human factor in man's salvation; it was not just alarm at the Reformer's radicalism which caused him to write his defence of free will against Lutheran determinism. And the idea that the More of the *Utopia* was a different man from the More of the tracts against Tyndale rests upon a misunderstanding of the aim of the earlier work, which was not designed to sketch an alternative to Catholicism, but rather a natural religion which represented the best to which human knowledge without the Christian revelation could attain. In so far as they are not *sui generis* the Catholic reforming group of the early sixteenth century in England are precursors of the Counter-Reformation humanism which Bremond has so attractively depicted in its French manifestations.

It must be remembered, too, that humanism influenced many scholars in England whose subsequent careers show the variety of religious opinions with which it could be combined. Besides the great triumvirate already mentioned, Pole, Tunstall, and, to a lesser extent, Gardiner were all lovers of humane letters. The first became the implacable opponent of Henry VIII's schism with much more vigour than More, who only asked liberty to follow his own conscience. The other two became supporters of the King's Supremacy and wrote in defence of it; after opposing the Edwardine Reformation, they returned to the Papal obedience under Mary, though hopes were entertained of Tunstall's accepting the Elizabethan settlement before his death, and he had shown himself loath to prosecute Protestants. The Cambridge Reformers grew up in a university which had been under the spell of Erasmus and was agitated about Greek studies. And it is worth recalling that Henry VIII himself and Katharine of Aragon were great promoters of humanism at their court. Humanism was the culture of the day and, if it was not without its effect upon the religion of all it influenced, that effect was far from uniform. Both Protestantism and Catholicism had their medieval and their Renaissance elements and it is a work of the utmost delicacy to distinguish between them in either case.

There was then no sharply defined party of Catholic Reformers. The opposition to Protestantism, like Protestantism itself, contained very diverse elements; one can distinguish a right and a left wing, mere conservatives on the one hand and those who thought the new religion a remedy worse than the disease it professed to cure on the other. But that is all. The Catholics with a zeal for reform would certainly have refused to be differentiated from other Catholics as regards basic principles; Sir Thomas More certainly did not think of himself as defending against Tyndale and his fellows his own private interpretation of Catholicism—however much he may have felt constrained to dissociate himself from the popular superstitions which had attached themselves to his faith—but rather as championing the religion of the vast majority of Englishmen.

Such then was the religious pattern of England just before the breach with Rome. A traditional faith which, though under attack from a minority for a century and more, was often not held very consciously; for it possessed a monopoly

and was so familiar as to be taken for granted. Nevertheless
men were not indifferent to it, but practised it with punctilious-
ness, if not in many cases with much thought, and sometimes
with too little idea of the link between piety and morals.
It was something deeply rooted in English history and the
very soil, something with such deep and unconscious roots
that we have to go to a country which has never known the
Reformation to find a parallel to-day. There is all the difference in the world between a self-conscious Catholicism
which has known competition, and perhaps persecution,
and one which has never been seriously challenged. The latter
gains both strength and weakness from its immunity, strength
in that it is undemonstrative and rarely fanatical, weakness
in that it too easily acquiesces in, or takes a cynical attitude
towards, abuses, with the result that, when revolution is in
the air, it finds little positive to propose as an alternative
to it. It has both the solidarity and the flimsiness of any
ancien régime. And in England the revolutionary elements
in religion had been developing with Lollardy under persecution and were now to be strengthened by a heady intoxicant
from Germany and later from Switzerland. At the same
time the almost inevitable conflict between Renaissance
absolutism in its characteristically English form and the
autonomous medieval church was to break out with un-
expected rapidity and, in so doing, to provide the revolutionaries eventually with the opportunity they sought.

3

The Regime of Wolsey and the Royal Divorce

BY COMMON CONSENT the period of Cardinal Thomas Wolsey's control of the English administration was later taken to be in one sense the precipitating cause of the English Reformation. Protestants looked back to his career as the supreme example of all they most detested in the old system, a display of *hubris* which provoked the Nemesis of collapse; Catholics thought of him as the unscrupulous prelate whose suggestion of the divorce scheme to the King for his own ends unleashed the disasters which were never to be permanently rectified. If both views are too simple, there is some truth in the main thesis they agree in maintaining. For Wolsey, by his very position as much as by his character, made starkly obvious the problem presented in the sixteenth century by the continuance of the medieval system of Church and State and at the same time unconsciously showed the way to one solution of it which would have horrified him if he had lived to see it.

To understand, one must appreciate the sources of Wolsey's unique position of authority, unparalleled hitherto in English history. A man of humble origins—his chief offence in the eyes of many of his enemies—he reached the royal service during Henry VII's reign by way of a successful Oxford career (during which he was Fellow and Bursar of Magdalen), and a position on the staff of the Deputy Lieutenant of Calais. By the time of Henry VIII's accession in 1509, however, he had reached no higher position in the royal household than that of a man found useful as a diplomatic underling. Thenceforth his rise was meteoric. Within little more than six months he was Royal Almoner and within two years one finds him a close confidant of the King, able to short-circuit even the cumbrous machinery of issuing State documents by a mere intimation of the royal will; by 1512 he is managing the French War and can be regarded as chief royal minister. Cavendish, his servant and biographer, is probably right in attributing his rise to the young king's dislike of routine.

The king was young and lusty, disposed all to mirth and pleasure, and to follow his desire and appetite, nothing minding to travail in the busy affairs of the realm. The which the almoner perceiving very well took upon him therefore to disburden the king of so weighty a charge and troublesome business, putting the king in comfort that he shall not need to spare any time of his pleasure, for any business that should necessarily happen in the council, as long as he, being there and having the king's authority and commandment, doubted not to see all things sufficiently furnished and perfected; the which would first make the king privy of all such matters as should pass through their hands before he would proceed to the finishing or determining of the same, whose mind and pleasure he would fulfil and follow to the uttermost, wherewith the king was wonderfully pleased.

So far there is nothing in Wolsey's position, except his all but monopoly of the royal favour, to distinguish him from many an earlier statesman-ecclesiastic of the Middle Ages. There was nothing new in a churchman steering the ship of state; it would have been impossible to find any English administration up till this time which did not include ecclesiastics—the indispensable ministers in an age when few laymen were educated. What was novel was the use that Wolsey now began to make of his dual capacity as an ordained man, capable of high office in the Church, and at the same time minister of state. By the end of 1515 he was Lord Chancellor of England and Cardinal Archbishop of York as well, that is to say the holder both of the traditionally highest post under the Crown and the incumbent of the second see in the English Church, as well as a Prince of the Roman

Church. Here too there were precedents; in the last reign Cardinal Morton had been both Lord Chancellor and Archbishop of Canterbury, an even more remarkable combination of great posts in Church and State. But Wolsey saw his way to make something new of the posts he had accumulated, to do no less than to couple together the English Church and the English State, with himself under the King at their head. The procedure was comparatively simple; all that was needed was to obtain from the Pope the rights of a legate of the Holy See *a latere*. A papal legate was the Pope's direct representative and, within limits, could exercise the Pope's authority within the area of his legacy. In England this had one important result: it meant that the Church of England for once could be treated as an ecclesiastical unity. In theory the medieval English Church had no existence as a canonical entity; it was no more than two provinces of the Universal Church, between which there was no more inherent connexion than between two provinces in different countries—the provinces of Rouen and Cologne for example. The honorific position of the Archbishop of Canterbury as Primate of All England gave him no authority over the Archbishop of York (as was emphasized by the latter's counter-title of Primate of England). But a papal legate represented the sovereign power in the Church and so could treat as one unit two separate parts of the Pope's sphere of jurisdiction; he could for example summon a national council of both provinces and his direct authority was equal in either of them.

Cavendish, whose mind ran upon precedence and display, represents his master's object in obtaining his legacy as a desire to spite Archbishop Warham of Canterbury, who had objected to Wolsey's use of his archiepiscopal cross in Warham's province. 'And York perceiving the obedience that Canterbury claimed to have of York, intended to provide some such means that he would rather be superior in dignity to Canterbury than to be either obedient or equal to him.' Though this may have been a motive, it is unlikely that the Cardinal limited his aims to the sole object of being above the senior Archbishop. However it certainly was the case that his new position had this result; by long-standing custom every Archbishop was *Legatus natus*, *ex officio* Legate of the Holy See. It was, however, a position which gave certain privileges of issuing dispensations and little more, and his legatine authority was automatically overruled by the presence of a legate *a latere*, much as is the authority of a permanent ambassador by the coming of a special envoy from the country which employs him. But the vital fact about Wolsey's position was that already mentioned, namely his supreme authority in both parts of the Church of England. It must be remembered too that his post as immediate representative of the Pope gave him power also over those monasteries which were normally free from the jurisdiction of either Archbishop, the exempt houses directly subject to Rome. There was in fact no corner of the English ecclesiastical framework to which Wolsey's power did not extend.

The method of obtaining such extensive powers from the Pope was simple but ingenious. In 1518 Leo X was endeavouring to raise a crusade against the Turks and wished to send Cardinal Campeggio (afterwards to play such a large part in the royal divorce suit) to promote it in England. He was informed that the laws of the realm normally forbade the reception of legates, but that the prohibition would be waived if Wolsey, the King's subject, were associated with the Italian as another legate on equal terms. It was thus that Wolsey obtained the position which, by constant pestering of Rome, he got extended both in powers and duration until in 1523 it was made a life appointment.

On the face of things the Wolsey period must have appeared to contemporaries as a dramatic assertion of papal power in England. For the King's chief minister also to be the direct representative and servant of the Pope, overriding the ordinary ecclesiastical authorities of the realm and appearing in public in the insignia of the Papal Curia, might well have seemed a return to the days of Henry III, when papal legates for a time ruled the land on behalf of the Pope, England's overlord. In fact a moment's reflection will show that the position was exactly reversed. Not only did Wolsey owe his power in

matters secular to the King's appointment; his position in
the Church was equally the result of the royal favour. Without that the Pope would never have given him the prefer-
ment which made him what he was ecclesiastically. In either
capacity Wolsey was ultimately the King's creature; he had
no authority which came from himself. 'It was,' says Dr.
Kenneth Pickthorn, 'the royal choice which raised the minister
to power and which kept him there: the minister was well
aware of this. and knew also that he was chosen for his
personal and not for any official or feudal or factious quali-
fications, that he had none of that strength of indispensability
which earlier and later ministers have had because they brought
to the service of the Crown ecclesiastical or territorial or
parliamentary resources which the Crown could neither do
without nor secure but by their mediation: Wolsey was more
powerful than Dunstan or the duke of Newcastle, than the
earl of Warwick or Sir Robert Cecil, more powerful against
all the world except the king, because he had all the king's
favour: but all his power came from that one source.' The
proof of this lies in the utter and irremediable nature of
Wolsey's fall once the King's favour was withdrawn.

In view of this, is it too fanciful for us to imagine that
Wolsey during his time of office taught Henry VIII—or
someone else with eyes to see, Thomas Cromwell for instance—two lessons of portentous significance? First, that
Church and State in England could be welded together to
form an engine of immense power from which no individual
in the realm could escape. Secondly, that, whereas this
combined organ of authority had been used by Wolsey
largely for non-national ends, it could be made a means of
national autarchy and aggrandizement. For Wolsey's policy
had done little to aid England at home or abroad. He was
little interested in England itself: 'Throughout the whole
period of his long administration,' says Brewer, the editor
of the documents relating to the period, 'and through all his
correspondence, it is remarkable how small a portion of his
thoughts is occupied with domestic matters.' The Cardinal
looked upon his country chiefly as a source of revenue to

finance a grandiose foreign policy. And this in turn, if Pollard is right, was directed wholly in the interests of the Holy See, which Wolsey more than once hoped to occupy. It was moreover a costly failure; at his fall Wolsey, after an expenditure which had nearly bankrupted the country and caused widespread discontent among the taxpayers, was clinging desperately to a precarious French alliance as England's one protection against the Emperor Charles V, then at the height of his power in Europe. Wolsey had used papal supremacy to unify authority in England under himself and the King and directed the power thus gained to ends in which England had little direct interest. Did not that give the idea for a royal supremacy which could use the same instrument for national purposes?

This is all the more probable in that Wolsey's fall resulted from his mismanagement, as Henry regarded it, of the royal marriage case, which showed that even a papal legate could not be relied upon to make the Pope in all things compliant with a king's desires. A legate was after all, however much also a royal servant, the deputy of an independent sovereign over whose actions a national king had no final control. Had Wolsey possessed absolutely plenary powers he would no doubt obediently have declared Henry's marriage with Katharine of Aragon invalid when asked. But he was a delegate, not a principal, and so great a matter as this was not within the sphere of his routine powers. Recourse had to be had direct to Rome and it was because of this that the 'king's great matter' failed.

To understand why, it is necessary to examine rather closely the issues involved. It should perhaps be unnecessary to state that the release from his wife which Henry demanded had nothing in common with what is commonly called a divorce suit in modern England. That claims to be the dissolution of a valid existing marriage, which by English statute law since 1857 can be granted by the High Court and earlier was sometimes effected by private Acts of Parliament. This however is an innovation brought about by a change of beliefs; in the sixteenth century the doctrine of the

Church that Christian marriage is indissoluble was universally accepted. No divorce in the modern sense was therefore possible. Nevertheless, since a marriage in order to be valid had to satisfy certain conditions, it was possible for a judicial investigation to prove that, owing to circumstances existing at the time of the ceremony, a particular marriage failed to satisfy those conditions and therefore, though mistakenly supposed to be so, had never really been a marriage at all. (It was to this form of process, or to that now known as 'judicial separation', that the term 'divorce' was in the language of the period applied.) This then was Henry's case: that Katharine had never been his lawful wife, since there had been at the time of marriage a circumstance preventing the union from being a binding, sacramental marriage according to the law of the Church. This once declared by ecclesiastical authority to be the case the King would be free to contract a new, and this time valid, match.

The circumstance alleged, in technical language the 'impediment', was that known in canon law as affinity. Katharine had been married to Prince Arthur, Henry's elder brother, and had espoused Henry after her first husband's death. But marriage, so it was held, because it made man and woman one flesh, made the husband's relatives relatives also of his wife, and conversely the wife's relatives her husband's. Henry and Katharine therefore stood to each other in a parallel relationship to that of brother and sister, so that, ordinarily speaking at least, marriage between them was unthinkable. This was realized of course at the time, but, as the second marriage was thought important for reasons of state, a way out was sought. Many impediments to marriage could be dispensed by the Pope in particular cases, for he was held to have the right (similar to the dispensing power claimed by English kings up to 1688 in respect of statute law) to set aside the provisions of a particular canon when circumstances seemed to justify it. But had he the power in this case? Some marriage impediments, it was agreed, had been made such merely by the law of the Church and what the Church had bound the Church, or its earthly Head, could loose. Others

however were held to be due to the revealed will of God,
which neither Church nor Pope could gainsay; thus no
ecclesiastical authority could permit the marriage of those
who stood in the closest degree of blood relationship (con-
sanguinity) though it might do so when it was a question of
a lesser degree. How did the matter stand in the case of
affinity, relationship constituted by marriage? Could the
marriage of brother- and sister-in-law be held to fall within
the dispensing power of the Pope or was the impediment
which ordinarily forbade it, and would make it invalid if
disregarded, one imposed by God over which the Pope had
no power? The matter had been disputed in the fifteenth
century and only at the end of it had the former opinion
come to be held. It was first acted upon in 1500, only four
years before Julius II permitted the marriage of Henry and
Katharine, and curiously enough the earlier case was in
Katharine's family, for the Pope then dispensed the impediment of affinity in order to allow the King of Portugal to
marry Katharine's sister Mary after the death of Isabella, an
elder sister who had been his first wife. So the argument
from precedent was not, so far as time went, a strong one,
and there could still be found canonists who would argue
that the Pope in dispensing in the second degree of affinity,
to use the technical phraseology, had exceeded his powers.
There was the loophole, so Henry thought, if he liked to use it.

Why he decided to try to avail himself of this possible
avenue of escape from a union which had lasted eighteen
years in 1527, when the King began his manœuvres, and had
been in its earlier stages idyllically happy, has long been
disputed. It is a well known fact that for some time Henry
had been violently in love with Anne Boleyn, the vivacious,
French-educated waiting lady of his wife. Was this his sole
motive? Since Henry had not been a faithful husband and
Mary, Anne's elder sister, had been one of his mistresses, the
theory would not in itself explain his anxiety to be free to
marry. But the fact that Anne, whose ambitious relations
formed a party round her, seems to have stood out for the
status of wife and at first refused her favours on any other

terms makes it more plausible. On the other hand one cannot consider the matter in isolation from the greatest problem of statecraft facing Henry at the time, that of the succession. The Tudors had come to the throne to restore order after a series of dynastic wars, the Wars of the Roses, occasioned by uncertainty and disputes about the descent of the Crown. These were still a relatively recent memory in 1527. And Henry had no male heir. Katharine had borne him one surviving daughter, Mary; all the rest of their children had been born dead or died soon after birth. The next heirs were collateral and the possibility of their succeeding would revive the doubts about the slender Tudor claim to the throne by heredity; it is easier to compete with a distant relative of a dead king than with his child. Even if Mary succeeded there was the question of her marriage—already being considered— and the problems it raised in the tangled state of European politics. Mary too might die before she had a child. Nor was there as yet any precedent for a female sovereign of England, except the unhappy one of Matilda, daughter of Henry I, over whose claims a civil war had been fought. There was then ample reason for the King to be sincerely worried about the future and there seemed no possibility of an alternative direct heir so long as Katharine remained his wife.

Henry's ostensible reason for approaching the Pope was his conscience; he had, he said, real doubt about the validity of his marriage, which prevented him from living with the Queen with a quiet conscience. It is easy to dismiss this as hypocrisy, but perhaps too easy. We have already noticed the peculiar connexion between Henry's conscience and his interests; but that fact does not disprove the existence and activity of the former. Self-deception is the easiest of human occupations. The King had been theologically trained and could appreciate the subtleties of the admittedly compli- cated circumstances connected with his specially dispensed marriage. Moreover the argument which could be used to deny the validity of the papal dispensation was one from Scripture; the Book of Leviticus had forbidden the marriage of a man with his brother's wife. Was not this law, of Divine origin, still binding under the New Covenant and, if so, how could the Pope set it aside? But the verse (Lev. xx. 21) ran thus: 'And if a man shall take his brother's wife, it is an unclean thing: . . . *they shall be childless.*' The application to the King's case seemed dramatically appropriate and might well strike a man already genuinely concerned about his lack of a suitable heir.

There is, then, no need to suppose that any single motive determined the decision of 1527: there were two substantial ones in Anne and the uncertain succession. Henry's conscience, odd as it may have been, could well have supplied a third, and must in any case have judged of the other two. Whether he acted in good faith or bad is a question which the historian cannot answer; the historical fact is that he acted. Whether the initiative was his is again a disputed question. It has been alleged that the Bishop of Tarbes, head of an embassy from France to arrange a marriage between the Princess Mary and the King of France, raised the issue of Mary's legitimacy as a bargaining point; it has also been said that Bishop Longland, the royal confessor, sowed doubts in Henry's mind at Wolsey's instigation. Both stories might be true; Wolsey was set upon a French alliance and saw in Katharine, who was for family reasons anti-French, an obstacle to it. The Cardinal could very well have made use of both bishops to advance his schemes, believing, in his overweening confidence, that his influence at Rome could carry through the divorce; certainly Katharine believed him to be the author of her misfortunes and she had means of knowing the intrigues of the Court. But in any case it is unlikely that the idea was first broached in 1527; for Henry must have been mediating some time earlier on a way of marrying the woman with whom he was in love.

The first steps had an air of comedy. Henry appeared by proxy before Wolsey as Legate and Archbishop Warham to answer a charge of living in sin with his brother's wife. Nothing came of this collusive suit, probably because it was realised that the value of a papal bull could not be impugned

except at Rome itself and that by long custom the marriage
affairs of princes, which had such wide repercussions, were
reserved to the Holy See in a special manner and could not,
like those of lesser men, be disposed of by local ecclesiastical
authorities. So began the long siege of Clement VII, designed
to make him pronounce the King an unconscious bachelor.

At this stage the matter became involved directly in the
international tangle of Europe. Katharine was no beggar-
maid Queen; she came of the royal family of Spain and was
the aunt of Charles V, Holy Roman Emperor, King of Spain
and lord in different ways of the greater part of Europe.
Charles had this very year stormed Rome itself and reduced
the Pope, his political enemy though his spiritual Father, to
submission. And, in spite of the efforts of the King's servants
to prevent it, Katharine had managed to inform her nephew
of what was happening. She was not therefore without an
ally and an influential one, half-hearted as he was to prove
at some stages of the business.

To follow the intricacies of the negotiations, which dragged
on for two years until the setting up of a legatine court to
try the case in England, would take too much space. Nor
are they significant for our purpose, except for the light
they throw upon underlying issues soon to come to the
surface.

In the earlier negotiations Henry did not raise the question
of the Pope's power to issue such a dispensation as that
which had made his marriage possible. He had, in his book
against Luther, spoken in strong terms of the Papal position
(in spite, ironically enough, of the advice of Sir Thomas
More to 'leave out that point, or else to touch it more slenderly') and it may well be that it was some time before he
came to the opinion that no Pope could allow a man to marry
his brother's wife. So the arguments put forward against
the validity of Julius's dispensation were technical ones relating
to the way in which it had been obtained, arguments which if
accepted would make the bull canonically invalid and the
marriage based upon it null and void. His chief anxiety
however was to get a commission from the Pope which

would allow the case to be finally decided in England in such a way as to leave Katharine no chance of appealing to the Pope in person from his representatives. This would not only avoid the indignity of the King's being summoned in a lawsuit outside his own dominions but would have the advantage of giving Wolsey a large share in the matter as legate, and Wolsey was the King's servant, who could be trusted to give the decision which would please his master. Clement, placed in a strait by fear of the anger of Charles V, delayed and hedged as much as possible. He made suggestions that the King should present him with a *fait accompli* by getting some kind of opinion in England against the validity of his original marriage and marrying again; it would be easier for the Pope to act if he was merely called upon to clear up a situation already in existence and not to create one which would seem an insult to the Emperor's aunt. But eventually, at the insistence of the King's envoy, Stephen Gardiner (later to be the famous Bishop of Winchester), he granted the commission. It was not in as full terms as Wolsey and Henry would have liked; it did not prevent the Pope from recalling the case to himself for final judgement if he saw fit, though he gave a verbal promise not to revoke the commission and to confirm the decision of his legates.

By the terms of this arrangement a court was to be set up in England to try the case under the presidency of Cardinals Wolsey and Campeggio. The latter, whom we have met before, had been asked for by the English government; holding as he did the English see of Salisbury, and knowing the country from his former visit, he was *persona grata*, as well as being a canonist of repute. Moreover he bore with him a further secret commission, the 'decretal commission' which settled the legal question in the case in advance and would reduce the task of the court to the mere ascertainment of facts—the document which Wolsey had all along wanted as the only way to settle the case beyond possibility of appeals and endless delay. The Pope had refused to grant it publicly, partly through fear of the Emperor and partly also through genuine concern for the reputation of the Holy See, which would then seem to be deciding the crux of the suit in advance after having heard one side only. But even now it was issued on condition that it should be shown to Henry and Wolsey alone and not be used in the hearing of the case. Moreover—and this only Campeggio knew—the Italian Cardinal was given private instructions to delay matters in every possible way, to try to find a way out by persuading Henry to take back Katharine, and not to give judgement until further orders. These instructions he carried out to the letter, but was forced finally to open his court in May 1529. In the meantime it was perceived that there were two strong points, not easily to be disposed of, in Katharine's case. Not only did she persist in asserting, as she had done all along, that her marriage with Prince Arthur had never been physically consummated—in which case canonically the impediment of affinity between her and Henry did not arise—but, more serious still, another document had turned up in the Spanish archives in which Julius II had given his dispensation for the marriage to Henry in much wider terms than in the text hitherto known—and the King's case turned largely upon the argument that the dispensation did not cover the facts as they really were. Henry's advisers declared the new find a forgery, but it was another matter to prove it so and the Pope refused to set it aside without the matter's being argued. A barefaced attempt to get the document to England and destroy it failed, and, as the Pope showed signs of revoking the case to himself, the King's party had to let matters proceed with their pleadings much less watertight than they had imagined. They were helped however by the Queen's determination not to submit to judgement in England; after appealing to the Pope and having her appeal disallowed by the legates she withdrew from the sessions of the court. Her counsel, all of whom except the saintly Bishop Fisher of Rochester were frightened of opposing the King, made a poor showing on her behalf. Campeggio who, however much he obeyed his orders to procrastinate, maintained a truly judicial frame of mind throughout and had rejected a suggestion from Rome that he should try to make Henry give way by threatening in advance to give sentence against his side, now wrote that if he judged strictly by what was laid before him he would be obliged to decide against the Queen. However he was spared this necessity by his masterpiece in the way of delaying action. When, at the session of 23 July, sentence was due to be pronounced, the Cardinal adjourned the court until October on the pretext that Roman courts were in vacation during this period (that of the heat of the Roman summer) and that a legatine court, though held in a colder climate, was bound by the same rule. It was his way of carrying out his instructions to make no decision without the Pope's further permission. Before October the Pope had revoked the suit to Rome. He was in a stronger position, on good terms with the Emperor and in no fear of England's ally, France, whose troops had just sustained a serious defeat in Italy. It was checkmate for Henry; he could never hope to get a sentence in his favour at Rome unless matters political changed very radically, and the very state of the European distribution of power deprived him of any means of putting pressure upon the Pope.

Checkmate—unless Henry was prepared to go a stage further. As yet he had acted, with whatever sharp practice, strictly within the limits of medieval orthodoxy. He had never questioned the Pope's authority, even whilst trying to rush or even bully him into granting what he wanted to satisfy his desires and secure the succession. He had not even overtly questioned Pope Julius's right to issue the dispensation, which was the fact upon which all turned in the suit. Even to do that would not necessarily take him outside the confines of Catholic doctrine as then understood; not even the most perfervid maximizer of the papal claims among theologians had ever claimed that there were no limits at all to papal powers, and it would not necessarily be heresy to claim that a particular Roman decision went outside them. Henry had based his scruples of conscience upon the verse of Leviticus which threatened childlessness to a union of brother- and sister-in-law—an attitude which must imply at least some doubt of the efficacy of a papal dispensation in such a case.

There is evidence that at least as early as 1529 he was wishing to find a theologian who would be prepared to maintain that affinity in the second degree was an impediment to marriage beyond the reach of the Pope's dispensing power.

But in fact Henry, through his envoys, had dropped even more drastic hints to Clement in the course of the negotiations which led to Campeggio's despatch to England. At the critical point, when Gardiner was pressing the Pope hard for the inclusion of the vital phrases he wanted in the commission to the two Cardinals, he reports using this threat to the Pope and his entourage:

I sayd, I thought it *Goddys wil* indede, to thintent relation made by us of what condition men be here towards them, *qui optima promeruerunt*, the favour of that Prynce, who now only favorith them, should be withdrawn, and taken away: *ut inclinata jam sedes apostolica tota corrueret, communi consensu atque applausu omnium.*

The narrative continues dramatically,

At these words the Popes Ho. casting his armes abrode, bad us put in the words we varyed for: and therwith walked up and down the chamber: casting now and then his armes abrode, we standing in a great silence.

In themselves Gardiner's words might mean no more than a threat of withdrawal of English political support from the Holy See in its parlous plight after the siege of Rome. But, with the experience of the effects of Luther's revolt in Germany, the Pope may well have seen in them, and been intended to see, a more radical significance. Gardiner had already said that 'papal laws which were highly uncertain even to the Pope and his servants might well be given to the flames'— perhaps an ominous reference to Luther's burning of the canon law at Wittenberg in 1520. When Campeggio reached England he was horrified to find Lutheran books in English circulating at the royal court and understood that in one the Lutherans promised 'to abrogate all the heresies respecting the articles of the Faith, and to believe according to the Divine law, provided that this King, with the most Christian King of France, England's ally, will undertake to reduce the ecclesiastical state to the condition of the primitive Church, taking from it all its temporalities'. In a conversation with Campeggio about this the King said significantly that the Lutherans claimed that these ideas had been arrived at by ecclesiastics themselves, and, when Campeggio tried to persuade him that if laymen got church goods they would be a danger to kings, went on to quote the Lutherans for the opinion that ecclesiastics, especially those of Rome, lived very wickedly. Campeggio admitted that there were spots on the Curia but claimed that the Holy See had never 'deviated a jot from the true faith'. The discussion ended with the King's assuring the Cardinal that he would always remain a good Christian but merely wished to convey what he had heard and would be glad if Campeggio would pass it on to Rome without quoting Henry as the source. The King of England could hint a threat more politely than his ambassadors.

There is evidence that the group behind Anne Boleyn, whether sincerely or not, were coquetting with Lutheranism and trying to influence the King in that direction. His court too had more than its share of the English anti-clerical feeling, as had been proved in 1515. Then, in the dispute about the rights of Church and State which arose out of the Hunne case, the secular lords and the judges came out strongly against the Abbot of Winchcombe, who had maintained in a sermon that a recent Act of Parliament, which limited clerical rights of immunity from secular justice, was an infringement of canon law. They made a hero of Dr. Standish, a Franciscan who was prepared to defend such encroachments upon the old liberties of the Church and even to hold that papal laws did not bind a country which had not expressly accepted them. The controversy was summed up by the King, who said: 'We are, by the sufferance of God, King of England, and the Kings of England in time past never had any superior but God; know, therefore, that we will maintain the rights of the crown in this matter like our progenitors.' The germs of the Royal Supremacy are already there in these words.

But Henry was slow to proceed to extremes; it was to be some years yet before the final irrevocable step which made

him a schismatic in the Pope's eyes. For the moment the
direct result of the rebuff received when Campeggio refused
his sentence and Clement withdrew the marriage case from
English soil was the fall of Wolsey. It was not only the royal
anger at the Cardinal's failure to get him what he so much
wanted which brought it about. There had been friction about
other matters between King and Chancellor and probably
Henry was already tiring of a servant who spoke of *Ego et
rex meus* and was popularly supposed to rule England. Anne
and the Boleyn faction hated Wolsey and they were now in
the ascendant. He was disliked and despised as an upstart
by the lay nobility and was feared and not loved by church-
men who had to suffer his arrogance as Legate. His foreign
policy had proved a failure and his French alliance, from
which so little had been gained, was making him more than
ever unpopular with the trading classes who, having had for
years to finance his adventures abroad by heavy taxation,
now feared his leading them into a war with the Emperor,
whose Flemish dominions were England's best customer.
He was ripe for removal and the failure of the 'King's matter'
did but precipitate his fall. In October 1529, he was indicted
in the King's Bench under the Praemunire laws for exercising
his legatine powers in such a way as to invade rights protected
by those laws and dismissed from the Chancellorship. He
escaped severer punishment by yielding up much of his vast
wealth to the King, and an attempt to condemn him in
Parliament by Act of Attainder was defeated by the arguments
of Thomas Cromwell in the Commons. Cromwell was
perhaps making a gesture of sympathy with his old master
but doubtless it was with the approval of the King, whose
service he was now entering. Wolsey retired to his see of
York and was preparing to play at last the part of an active
diocesan bishop and metropolitan. But in November 1530,
he was arrested on a charge of high treason for seeking the
intercession of the King of France with Henry and died at
Leicester Abbey on his way south for trial.

His end marked the close of an epoch in English history
as, in a lesser sense, his rise had been the beginning of one.

Last of the great English ecclesiastical statesmen of the Middle Ages, he had been, in his amphibious and paradoxical position, at once servant of King and Pope, maintaining by means of this fact an illogical concentration of the power of Church and State, a living anomaly. His fall and death, at the very moment at which the old system he represented and yet had transformed was reaching an obvious crisis, was both a portent and an event which set the stage for the revolution which was now to begin and gather momentum.

4

The Subjugation of the Church

IT IS DIFFICULT TO KNOW how far the policy upon which Henry VIII embarked after the dismissal of Wolsey was from the first a connected plan, intended to be realized by stages. Looked at in the light of later events its earlier stages seem like the first steps of a planned offensive aimed at what was finally secured, namely the concentration of all ecclesiastical power, legislative, judicial, and administrative, under the control of the King. And all that one knows of the mind of Thomas Cromwell, who was the chief royal agent during the vital stages of the revolution effected by the Crown, inclines one to believe that he at least may have had a detailed plan of campaign in his head from the beginning. Yet there are sufficient elements of tentativeness in what was done to make one doubtful of how far the King intended to go, and it is on the whole unlikely that he envisaged the complete breach with Rome which actually occurred, and all its consequences, as early as the end of 1529. Like most revolutionaries he was driven forward by the pressure of events, once he had determined to have his way in the matter which occupied the forefront of his mind at that date, namely the annulment of his marriage and the making of Anne Boleyn Queen.

The first action taken has about it a flavour both of revenge for the King's humiliation at the hands of the Church and of resolve to reassert the rights of the English Crown in the ecclesiastical affairs of its realm. It is interesting to notice both these things coming out as early as October 1529.

Campeggio, returning to Rome, had had his baggage searched by royal officials at Dover. He complained of this as an insult to his position as Legate. A letter in reply (probably composed by Gardiner, who was now the King's Secretary) told him that his legateship had ceased with the revocation of the cause to Rome. 'I am astonished,' ran the letter, 'that you are so ignorant of the laws of this realm as to dare to make use of the title of Legate, to which you have no longer any right, for you are a bishop of this realm and you are bound by the most solemn obligation to pay due regard and respect to my royal dignity, my jurisdiction and prerogative.' The obedience to which Henry laid claim, even from a Cardinal Bishop of Salisbury, before whom he had but recently appeared as a suppliant, he was going all the more to enforce from the other ecclesiastics of the realm.

In the summer of 1530 writs of Praemunire were issued in King's Bench summoning fifteen clerics (including eight bishops) to answer charges of having been fautors and abettors of Wolsey's legateship, by making agreements with him to pay him part of their annual income probably in order to prevent his interference with their ecclesiastical jurisdiction. (It is possible that these fifteen were singled out because most of them had in one way or another supported Queen Katharine in the divorce suit.) This case never came to a conclusion because by the next year it had been subsumed in a more general attack upon the whole body of the clergy whom the King, apparently after some debate in Parliament, accused, by a message to Convocation, of violating the Statutes of Provisors and Praemunire in the exercise of their spiritual jurisdiction. It was not, as used to be thought, their recognition of Wolsey's authority which was the basis of this general accusation and it would seem that the King was, even as early as this, laying a claim that the ultimate cure of the souls of his subjects was committed to him, so that any exercise of spiritual jurisdiction independent of his authority could be illegal. He offered pardon in return for a clerical subsidy eventually fixed at £100,000, but later made it a condition that the money must be accompanied by an acknowledgement that he was 'Protector and Supreme Head of the English Church and Clergy'. The practical effect of this title was not at this time defined, but the clergy were evidently perturbed by its implications and managed to get the expression modified to 'especial Protector, single and supreme Lord, and, as far as the law of Christ allows (*quantum per Christi legem licet*), even Supreme Head', a compromise even voted only by a *nemine contradicente* silence at the appeal of Archbishop Warham. The King's retreat was, however, rather more substantial than used to be thought, for, in their acknowledgement, the clergy managed also deftly to alter the suggestion that the King had the cure of souls and to ignore his sinister suggestion that he would confirm the ancient privileges and liberties of the English Church in so far as they were not contrary to his royal power and the laws of the realm, although they were not able to secure a guarantee for which, they had asked, that Praemunire should be more precisely defined by Parliament so that they might not unwittingly violate its provisions again. In the Convocation of York, to which the King's demands were passed on for parallel action, the matter was held up for months by the opposition of Cuthbert Tunstall, then Bishop of Durham and its president during the vacancy of the Archbishopric of York, and in the end was passed against his vote and with a formal protest by him in the records. (The incident is interesting in view of Tunstall's later career as a supporter of the Royal Supremacy; the 'Henrician' bishops were a party converted by fear.)

The King had now got a document which could be used as a fulcrum against the clergy should Henry want to make further demands later, even if he had not been granted all that he originally demanded. It may well be, as Dr. Scarisbrick, who has unravelled the whole complicated story, suggests, that Henry in 1531 was concerned more to intimidate the Pope, from whom he still hoped for a settlement of the marriage case in his favour, by a threat of destroying the independence of the English Church, and to obtain money, than actually to begin establishing a royal supremacy at once, as he was later to do. But the extent of his demands shows how his mind was moving and the vital fact was that the Crown had been formally declared an essential part of the constitution of the Church in England.

For the time being policy was still determined by the exigences of the divorce suit, in which the King still did not despair of wrenching a favourable verdict from Rome. In August 1529 a new method of procedure had been adopted upon the suggestion of a figure who now for the first time becomes a personage outside Cambridge academic circles in which he had previously moved, Thomas Cranmer. Meeting by chance Gardiner and Foxe, who were still the King's agents for the suit, Cranmer suggested to them that the real issues in Henry's case were theological rather than merely canonical, and could be better decided by the judgements of divines than by ecclesiastical courts. (This fitted in with an idea already canvassed by the King's advisers of obtaining learned opinions from the universities of Europe which might be effective in doing what diplomatic pressure upon the Papacy had failed to to.) The idea was reported to the King, who was attracted by it, and Cranmer's rapid rise into royal favour, which was to bring him soon to the see of Canterbury, dated from this time. In view of the theological uncertainties already mentioned which were involved in the dispensation under which Henry had been married, it is easy to see the merits of Cranmer's plan, though the way in which it was implemented by the royal agents was not very creditable. Intimidation and fraud were used to get favourable opinions from Oxford and Cambridge. Outside the realm direct force could not be used, but Francis I, Henry's ally, brought pressure to bear upon the French universities and bribery was used in the Italian academies. Henry's opponents were equally anxious to get opinions in their favour rather than objective judgements, as is shown by the unanimity of the Spanish universities in favour of Katharine. And the fact that there was something to be said for the King's case is shown by the verdicts given for him by, for example, Bologna (the great legal school which lay in papal territory) and

Padua, another school of distinction. In all, Henry had a respectable body of learned opinion, whatever its sources, to send to the Pope, when the collection was complete. It was forwarded in 1530 and in July a great petition signed by a number of notables of the realm (including the fallen Wolsey) was sent in its support, though the King had to deal separately with each signatory to rake together enough names, and the Imperial Ambassador believed that if they had been asked in a body most would have refused. The tone used to the Pope was respectful, but the document had a sting in its tail. 'This if you will not do, if you who ought to be our father have determined to leave us orphans, and to treat us as castaways, we shall interpret such conduct to mean only that we are left to care for ourselves, and to seek our remedy elsewhere.' The Pope replied in September, in effect refusing the request, and saying, no doubt with irony in view of what he must have known of the origins of the petition, that the King could not have known of it and would read it with regret.

Henry's object at this time was to obtain his divorce by ecclesiastical authority with the Pope's acquiescence and by this means to avoid both the indignity and probable ill-success attached to pleading his cause at Rome. Archbishop Warham, displaying that intermittent firmness he could sometimes command, refused to flout the Pope's prohibition by hearing it in his own court, and Katharine refused to agree to any idea of a trial on neutral soil. It is this fact which explains more than anything else Henry's anxiety to reduce the English Church to submission to his will as quickly as possible, in order that he might from it obtain ultimately some judgement in his favour which would satisfy his not over-exacting conscience, and enable him to represent the new marriage, upon which he was determined, as sanctioned by something more than his mere will. He was already growing impatient and in the middle of 1531 produced a partial *fait accompli* by removing Katharine from court.

In the next stage of the siege against ecclesiastical independence the Government worked through Parliament. The Parliament summoned in 1529, just after the fall of

Wolsey, was destined to be the great 'Reformation Parliament' of English history and remained in being until 1536 by repeated prorogations—an unprecedented duration for such a body. The King saw the advisability of taking the nation along with him, as far as he could, in the policy to which he was becoming more and more committed, and Parliament was the only and the best means open to him both of trying to present a national united front to the hostile or critical outside world and of commending his proceedings to the nation at large. Sir Thomas More at his trial spoke of this assembly in bitter words, when he claimed that for his opponents' one parliament, 'and God knows what manner of Parliament', he had on his side the general councils of a thousand years. His words are only one expression of an opinion, held both by contemporaries and men of later ages, that it was a packed body. (Thus, the chronicler Hall, a great admirer of Henry VIII, says that 'the most part of the Commons were the King's servants'.) It is a well-known fact that the Crown did not scruple in the sixteenth century to use all the influence in its power to sway elections to the House of Commons in its favour; nor did Henry VIII hesitate to intimate on occasion to hostile members of the House of Lords that they should not obey their writs of summons. It must however be remembered that the King at this date emphatically governed, and did not merely reign, and that such proceedings and the pressure exercised during sessions upon the Houses do not differ entirely from the efforts of a modern Cabinet to win a general election or to keep in being their majority in the legislature, without which government would be impossible. And it is scarcely more than a century since those ends have ceased to be attained by such practices as borough-mongering, bribes and threats. Tudor methods were crude and are indefensible by modern standards of constitutionalism, but they were not unconstitutional according to the ideas of the day. It would be dangerous to regard the Reformation Parliament as wholly unrepresentative of the opinions of the country, even though it was weighted on the King's side. And indeed Henry had more than once to use cajolery and even threats to force his measures through. The fundamental fact was that England as a whole, though by no means in favour of the King's proceedings, was not prepared to oppose him actively; the memories of the fifteenth century made the country prefer strong government, even if it offended their traditional ideas, to a situation in which faction could have full play.

Moreover, as has been said before, there was a strong practical anti-clericalism in the country, especially among the classes alone directly represented in the Commons, royal officials, country gentry, and town burgesses. It was upon this fact that Thomas Cromwell, now directing the royal policy, relied when, in January 1532, he had brought forward in the Commons a petition to the King against the Ordinaries of the realm. It was a long statement of the grievances felt by laymen against the ecclesiastical jurisdiction to which they had to submit in daily life, and more especially against the ways in which it was exercised. It was an ingenious plan; though the document was drawn up under official auspices (as various drafts of it, three of them with Cromwell's own corrections on them, show), it embodied sufficiently the grievances against the Church felt by the ordinary man to make it acceptable to a large part of the Commons. (It is possible that the original basis of the petition may have been complaints voiced against the Church in the Parliament of 1529.) The complaints were exaggerated, but there was enough truth in them to make a case. Moreover—and this was its usefulness from the Government's point of view— it contained requests that the clergy should not in future be allowed to make new canons without the King's assent and that the existing canon law should be brought into conformity with the laws of the realm. It was an ideal instrument with which to attack the legislative independence of the Church.

At the same time the policy which was designed to obtain if possible the divorce decree from the Pope was advanced by the first of the anti-papal Acts of Parliament of Henry's series, that for the Conditional Restraint of Annates. Annates were the payments demanded by the Holy See of the first year's revenue of a bishopric by the person appointed to it. The payments had been felt as a grievance before: an Act of 1404 had complained of them and laid down that they were not to be raised above the customary level, and the topic had been raised in 1528 at Rome when the divorce negotiations were in process. The object of this new bill was to threaten Rome with the cutting off of one of its sources of English money, and for that purpose its effect was made conditional upon the failure of friendly negotiations with the Curia to secure the abolition of Annates, whilst in any case the Act was to become law only if the King within a limited time signified his wish that it should do so. Moreover it had comparatively little in it that could be regarded as a direct attack upon Papal authority; the Pope was mentioned in respectful terms, there was an emphatic declaration of the orthodoxy and Catholicity of the realm and the ordinary method of appointing bishops by papal bull was still allowed to continue. Only if the Pope in revenge declined to issue the necessary documents was there to be any departure from accepted custom; then the chosen bishop was to have his election confirmed by the Metropolitan and be consecrated, and if this procedure was met by Rome with interdict or excommunication the censure was to be disregarded. The idea is plain; the new Act was a bargaining, or, if one likes, a blackmailing, weapon presented to the King to use or not at his pleasure. If there was any idea of trying to make it appear to state a grievance of the English prelates, who were the direct sufferers from Annates, it was a failure, for all the bishops and abbots in the Lords voted against it. Nor did it pass the Commons without difficulty. But it could be, and was, represented by Henry as due to an outburst of indignation by his people which he could not control; the method will be recognized by all familiar with modern totalitarian methods of propaganda.

The petition asked the King to take action about these matters and he accordingly transmitted it to Convocation, when it met in April. That body must have had some idea that this was part of a concerted attack upon the clergy, for in

February Warham had made a formal protest 'against all enactments made in the parliament commenced in the Black-friars, 3 November 1529, in derogation of the Pope's authority, or of the ecclesiastical prerogative of the province of Canter-bury,' and a series of Acts, restricting benefit of clergy, re-straining citations in spiritual courts, and limiting grants of land to ecclesiastical corporations, had been passed at the same time as the Annates Act. Convocation's reply therefore to the Supplication against the Ordinaries, while polite, was unbending, though the first draft of it was toned down as being too stiff. It admitted that there were abuses in ecclesi-astical procedure, but it denied some of the specific charges made by the Commons, and promised redress where good reason could be shown. But upon the essential right of the Church to unfettered legislative power it was rigid. The Ordinaries claimed that their power was of divine origin and could not therefore be surrendered. 'We say that forasmuch as we repute and take our authority of making of laws to be grounded upon the Scripture of God and the determination of Holy Church, which must also be a rule and square to try the justice and righteousness of all laws, as well spiritual as temporal, we verily trust that in such laws as have been made by us or by our predecessors . . . there shall be found nothing contained in them but such as may be well justified by the said rule and square.' Therefore their answer to the demand that they should seek the royal assent to canon law is a simple *non possumus*. 'We, your most humble subjects, may not submit the execution of our charge and duty, certainly pres-cribed by God, to your highness's assent.'

The King returned the answer to the Commons with a broad hint that they were not expected to find it satisfactory. 'We think their answer will smally please you, for it seemeth to us very slender.' He added with some hypocrisy: 'You be a great sort of wise men, I doubt not but you will look circumspectly on the matter, and we will be indifferent between you.' The King demanded a further reply from the clergy; this maintained no less strongly the inherent right of the Church to legislate without the consent of the temporal power, but retreated a little by offering as an act of grace to submit new canons for the royal approval and to suspend their operation until it was given. Also, the clergy would revoke any canons which were contrary to the royal prerogative and the laws of the realm, provided they did not concern Christian faith and morals. But the King was resolved upon total submission and now peremptorily demanded Convocation's promise of three things: first, that they would pass no new canons without his consent, secondly, that a mixed committee of clerics and laymen should examine the canon law of the English provinces with a view to seeing what parts of it ought to be abolished, and thirdly, that, after these had been weeded out, the remaining corpus should be established by the King's assent.

His ultimate reason for the demand he gave to a deputation of the Commons which he summoned to meet him. To them he made this speech:

Well-beloved subjects, we thought that the clergy of our realm had been our subjects wholely, but now we have well perceived that they be but half our subjects, yea and scarce our subjects: for all the prelates at their consecration make an oath to the pope clean contrary to the oath that they make to us, so that they seem to be his subjects and not ours: the copy of both the oaths I deliver here to you, requiring you to invent some order that we be not thus deluded of our spiritual subjects.

The 'discovery' was as opportune as most of Henry's seeings of the light, for it had never occurred to anyone hitherto that obedience to the Papacy was incompatible with civil obedience. But in fact Henry was reasoning from a new premise, the Renaissance conception of absolute unitary sovereignty which could brook no rivals—a contradiction of all medieval notions of the separate origins and rights of the spiritual and temporal powers and a return to the pagan Roman idea of *imperium*. It is the conflict between these two ideas which underlies most of the disputes of the English Reformation and which, unacknowledged, made the problem of liberty and toleration insoluble by most post-Renaissance political science. We see here the contrast between the medieval world and the modern in its sharpest form on the political side and it opens problems which are still with us.

For the moment nothing came of this last move, for an outbreak of plague caused the prorogation of Parliament. The contest with the clergy was brought swiftly to an end by a parallel prorogation, before which they had to make up their minds, and on 16 May they gave the King the document called the Submission of the Clergy, which granted his demands with little modification, passed by them the day before. Thus the right of legislation independently of the State was given up by the Church of England. Nothing had as yet been said about the far greater bulk of canon law which rested upon papal authority or upon that of general councils; the turn of that would come later. But the Convocations henceforward stood to the King in very much the same relation as did the Houses of Parliament. They could debate and they could make proposals; but the royal assent, and only the royal assent, could give their acts the force of binding law. It was the beginning of the Royal Supremacy.

The further stages by which that new principle of the English constitution was forged were determined by the progress of the divorce suit. The King's immediate aim in establishing his authority over the English clergy was undoubtedly to clear a way to securing from them a declaration of the invalidity of his marriage which would serve as an alternative, if an inferior one, to that he had hoped for from the Pope. For Clement remained obdurate, despite the opinions of universities, the petitions of English grandees, and even the threat to cut off Annates. Already Henry had been speaking fairly openly of the possibility of a schism from him. He had told Tunstall in a letter that he was 'informed by virtuous and learned men that, considering what the Church of Rome is, it is no schism to separate from it and adhere to the words of God'. He was in fact playing with Lutheranism to the extent of professing to doubt the divine origin, and even the legitimacy, of the papal prerogatives, though his progress to his final position of denying them was slow. But the practical issue of being free to marry

Anne, and secure the succession as he hoped, was immediate.

He was helped in his schemes by the death of Archbishop Warham in August 1532. The old Primate, vacillating and weak as he had often proved, was yet a strong adherent of the old order: as late as the May before his death he had maintained that the spiritual power of the archbishops did not depend upon the power of the prince and that the contrary proposition was against God's law. It was the surrender he was forced to make by the Submission of the Clergy which seems to have been one of the causes of his death, for he died broken-hearted. Now was Henry's opportunity; he could, if he played his cards well, secure a Primate of All England in sympathy with the new conception of royal authority and ready to defy the Pope. The man was available —Thomas Cranmer, who had already proved so useful. Henry probably knew that Cranmer's ideas went much further in the direction of Lutheranism than the King himself was ever ready to go; all through their association Henry, with his capacity for using for his own purposes men who did not agree with him or with each other, was to tolerate and protect in Cranmer what would have brought other men in danger of the King's wrath. But to have an Archbishop more radical than himself would be no bad thing; he would not have to drive a reluctant partner but at most to restrain a too eager ally. Above all Cranmer's views upon the divorce problem were well known. But for him to be of any use he must be in a canonically unquestioned position as Archbishop, and that still involved the consent of Rome. (It must always be remembered that from Henry's point of view a declaration of nullity carrying papal authority was the ideal. Only that could compel the assent of foreign powers in a way that one emanating from puppet English ecclesiastics could not do.) So, with effrontery one cannot but admire, Henry demanded bulls for his appointment, which the Pope in spite of many warnings, unwisely issued. The little matter of the oath to the Holy See, which the King had recently found so intolerable, was got over by an expedient in accordance with the manners of the age, though of doubtful

moral validity seen *sub specie aeternitatis*: Cranmer took the
oath, having previously made legal reservations in advance
that it should not bind him to do anything even apparently
against the law of God or the King and laws of England,
and that he was left free to consult and devise for the reformation of religion and the government of the Church of
England. When, at his trial in 1555, Dr. Martin examined
him upon this point and exclaimed, 'Hearken, good people,
what this man saith. He made a protestation one day to keep
never a whit of that which he would swear the next day,'
the Archbishop's sole reply was: 'That which I did, I did
by the best learned men's advice I could get at that time'.
The reply suggests some subsequent doubts of conscience,
but in 1533 it was Henry's conscience that was predominant
and that could easily have been set at rest by the plan that
was adopted. There is no need to doubt the truth of Cranmer's
further plea at his trial that 'there was never man came more
unwillingly to a bishoprick than I did to that', so much so
that when summoned from Germany, where he was on
diplomatic business for the King, he prolonged his journey
home by seven weeks in the hope that the King would forget
him. But the accusation then made—'that there was a compact between you, being then queen Anne's chaplain, and the
king: "Give me the archbishoprick of Canterbury, and I
will give you leave to live in adultery" '—was a not unnatural conclusion from this incident and the events that
followed. Though Cranmer was innocent of any such peculiarly
unpleasant simony as was suggested, his first duty in Henry's
intention was precisely to give sentence in the marriage case.

It is in the light of this, as much as of the more general
aspects of the matter, that we must see the legislation which
follows. By now time was pressing upon Henry. The future
Queen Elizabeth was born on 7 September, 1533, and therefore Henry and Anne Boleyn must have been living together
since at least January of that year and probably earlier. In
that month they had been secretly married. But that marriage,
which had anticipated any sentence of nullity upon Henry's
first union, must somehow be formally declared valid before

Anne's child was born, if the succession to the throne was to be assured. And in order to do that—since, despite slightly more friendly negotiations between Henry and Clement which partly explain the Pope's willingness to accept Cranmer, no remedy was in sight from Rome—much had to be changed in existing law. Henry, like Hitler in recent times, had a great belief in the magic effect of law created by himself as a justification of his acts. So he set himself to create a situation in which his cause could receive the authorization he wanted, and which would also greatly strengthen the position of the English Crown in ecclesiastical affairs. It is this which explains the Act in Restraint of Appeals which was passed by Parliament, not without much opposition, in February. It begins with the well-known passage which states in formal terms the theory upon which Henry VIII ever after acted:

Where by divers sundry old authentic histories and chronicles it is manifestly declared and expressed that this realm of England is an empire [i.e., a territory whose ruler is subject to no higher human power], and so hath been accepted in the world, governed by one supreme head and king, having the dignity and royal estate of the imperial crown of the same, unto whom a body politic, compact of all sorts and degrees of people, divided in terms and by names of spiritualty and temporalty, be bounden and ought to bear, next to God, a natural and humble obedience: he being also institute and furnished, by the goodness and sufferance of Almighty God, with plenary whole and entire power pre-eminence authority prerogative and jurisdiction to render and yield justice and final determination to all manner of folk . . . in all causes . . . without restraint or provocation to any foreign princes or potentates.

After this enunciation of this theory of Church and State finding their point of union in the King as Head of both, the Act goes on to explain that the spiritualty, or Church of England, has always been reputed of sufficient learning and authority to settle any matters of the Divine Law without 'the inter-meddling of any exterior person'. It then rehearses the inconveniences and troubles which had arisen by appeals to Rome in spiritual matters, and goes on to enact that matrimonial, testamentary, and tithe cases shall go no further than the Archbishop's court, except—a significant exception in view of what was shortly to come—in cases touching the King, when the Upper House of Convocation finally decides.

If, in its actual provisions, this law does not seem to go much beyond what Henry II had attempted in the Constitutions of Clarendon of 1164 and had stated to be merely a renewal of the old customs of the realm, it was in fact widely different from anything which had gone before, simply in virtue of the theory from which it proceeds. The Angevin king had merely wished to see that appeals did not go to Rome without his permission: the Tudor denied Rome's competence in spiritual causes and later was to claim it for himself. So, even if the enacting portion of the Act did not measure up to the sweeping claims of its preamble, yet Pickthorn may well speak of it as 'the most important of the sixteenth century, if not of any century', for, as he says, it 'robbed Rome of all jurisdiction: the frontier was not pushed back, it was wiped out, as if it had never existed really, never been part of an universal dispensation but only of a pretension which was local and secular ... This particular law was purporting to *make* nothing, only to establish what had once been, what should always have been, and what alone properly was.' In essence it contains what was to become the basis of the English Reformation, only to be broken in the revolt of consciences against State-made religion in the seventeenth century, the theory that the English Crown could determine the religion of England in general and in particular, according to its own interpretation of the Christian revelation.

For the moment, however, Henry probably had few such far-reaching ideas in the front of his mind. The immediate usefulness of the Act to him was seen in the very next month, when he induced Convocation to declare, first, that it was against the law of God for a man to marry his brother's widow when the previous marriage had been consummated, and secondly that the marriage between Katharine and Prince Arthur *had* been consummated. Both law and fact being thus prejudged and all appeal debarred, the way was open for Cranmer to give the formal judgement. He was solemnly licensed at his own request as 'the most principal minister of our spiritual jurisdiction within this our realm' by the plaintiff in the suit to judge it. Katharine, as was to be expected, refused to obey his summons and was pronounced contumacious (though the fact that sentence was to be pronounced was carefully kept from her, lest she should after all put in an appearance and complicate the suit), and on 23 May the Archbishop declared her second marriage null and void from the beginning. (By a most curious anomaly, of a type not uncommon in English history, Cranmer used in his definitive judgement his title of 'Legate of the Apostolic See' to which, as explained earlier, every Archbishop of Canterbury had an *ex officio* right; whether this was force of habit or is evidence that Henry even now did not contemplate a permanent breach with Rome, as some later indications suggest may have been the case, it is now impossible to say.) The nullity decree was followed by one declaring the validity of the marriage with Anne, who was forthwith crowned as Queen of England. The inevitable papal riposte was not long in coming; this was rebellion, both doctrinal and practical, and Rome could deal with it in only one way. In July Clement declared Anne not to be Henry's wife and simultaneously excommunicated the King, the effect of the sentence being suspended until September, in case the King should repent and put away his new partner. Two days before the pontifical sentence Henry had put into effect the Annates Act. His reply to the excommunication was the time-honoured one of appeal to a general council of the Church—a measure which would have increased his offence in the Pope's eyes, since Pius II in the last century had declared such appeals heretical. The breach with Rome was formal at last, and at the same time the decisive steps had been taken to subject the English Church to royal control. 'There are two kingdoms in Scotland,' Andrew Melville was later to say to James VI of that country, explaining that in one the King was vassal and not head; henceforward there was to be only one in England.

5
Consolidation and the Crushing of Opposition

A REVOLUTION only begins when it is declared; the settlement of a new constitution and the stamping out of counter-revolution is the longer, and commonly the harder, task. The years between 1533 and 1540 were to be occupied with this phase in the English ecclesiastical *bouleversement* formally inaugurated in the former year. It was a dangerous, and at times a bloody business, for, as in most of such cases, what opposition there was had been taken almost by surprise by the speed of the *Machtübernahme* and took some time to develop any resistance. In fact, however, there was little overt opposition, and no active resistance, before the Pilgrimage of Grace. This was due to several factors, primarily perhaps to the skill with which the King knew how to play upon anti-clerical prejudices, making refusal to accept his new order appear the championship of an effete and tiresome tyranny, but also to the thoroughness with which Thomas Cromwell and his agents used propaganda and unspectacular pressure to disarm possible revolt. One has to allow too for the powerful and, to modern minds, absurdly exaggerated deference to kingship in the sixteenth century, which approached idolatry in the case of Cranmer and other devotees of the secular power, and was active even in those, like Sir Thomas More, who were m : conscientiously opposed to the royal proceedings. Both in theory, and because they feared above all things a return to fifteenth-century faction, men were reluctant to criticize the King or to divide the national unity. There was to the end intense sympathy with Katharine's misfortunes, but it was chivalrous and verbal only, and there was no disposition to take up arms for her. Chapuys kept assuring Charles V that even a token invasion by Imperial forces would gain overwhelming support in England, but like all foreigners he did not understand the English temperament and his thinking was wishful.

First of all, however, came the legal consolidation of the new regime. It was accomplished chiefly by a series of Acts passed by Parliament in the first months of 1534. The legislature began where it had left off the previous year by passing a new and this time definitive Act against Annates. This made the former prohibition of their payment to Rome permanent and went on to forbid any Papal share in the making of bishops, who were henceforth to be elected by cathedral chapters as the canon law required on the receipt of the royal *congé d'élire*. But this did not mean freedom of election, any more than the previous system had done: the permission to elect was to be accompanied by letters missive nominating for election the person of the King's choice for the see, and failure to obey these was punishable by the penalties of Praemunire—and ineffective too, for the King could then appoint by letters patent alone. Thus royal control of episcopal appointments, practically complete before the schism, was made theoretically so by statute. Another Act cut off another source of Papal income, the traditional 'Peter's pence' paid since Anglo-Saxon times, and at the same time provided for the gap in Church administration caused by the impossibility henceforth of asking for or obtaining dispensations from Rome, which had become necessary for the day-to-day working of the cumbrous canonical system. They were to be issued in future by the Archbishop of Canterbury, who was to follow the traditional practice of the Roman Curia, and was to be subject to the control of the Crown in all matters of importance arising out of these documents. At the same time the exempt monasteries and other papal 'peculiars' were placed under the jurisdiction, not of the Archbishop, but of the King. The

Act contained a suspensive clause enabling the King either
to put it into effect or annul it as he liked—an indication that
Henry had not finally burnt his boats. Negotiations with the
Pope were in fact still going on, through the good offices of
the King of France, but how far Henry's delay was due to real
hopes of a settlement, and how far to common politeness to
Francis I, it is difficult to say. Henry was an opportunist
and a good offer from the Pope might not have been refused,
but he was now well embarked upon a revolutionary policy
and would probably in such a case have bargained for the
retention of some of his new powers over the English Church
as the price of reconciliation.

In any case nothing came of these last contacts. On 23
March Clement had at long last brought to an end the suit
which had begun in 1529 and solemnly pronounced for the
validity of Henry's first marriage. *Roma locuta erat* and there
could be no going back on the original cause of dispute.
The royal reply was to put into effect the Act against Peter's
Pence. Moreover, doctrinal, and not merely administrative,
action was being taken against papal claims. The Act just
mentioned had asserted that the King and his people did
not by it intend 'to decline or vary from the congregation of
Christ's Church in any things concerning the very articles of
the Catholic faith of Christendom', but it was clear that these
articles would in future be defined according to royal and not
papal standards. Throughout his reign Henry for the most
part maintained strict medieval orthodoxy in his dominions,
by the death penalty if necessary, but very often on grounds
which the Middle Ages would have considered heretical
private judgement. This was made clear by the Heresy Act
passed in this same session, which repealed the statute of
Henry IV's reign, under which heretics were to be burnt
upon mere conviction by the Church acting under canonical
procedure, and instead confirmed two Acts of Richard II's
and Henry V's time which laid down the procedure the Church
must follow before the State would burn a heretic. Not only
was persecution thus put under civil control, but the old
definition of heresy (which amounted practically to the

doctrine that whoever dissented from the teaching of the Roman Church was a heretic) was abandoned, on the ground that many heresies 'declared and ordained in and by the said canonical sanctions and by the laws and ordinances made by the popes or bishops of Rome' were 'but human'. The reason for this was that some things held by Rome to be heresy were now official doctrines of the law of England. The real meaning of this provision can be seen later in the statute, where it was quite unhistorically stated that the ordinance of the Bishop of Rome 'not approved and confirmed by holy scripture, was never commonly accepted or confirmed to be any law of God or man within this realm'. Therefore it was henceforth to be legal to speak against the Pope at will without incurring a charge of heresy, and to criticize his decrees. Where real heresy began was left undefined.

Another indication of the character of the new system was given by the Act for the Submission of the Clergy, which gave statutory force to the promises extracted from Convocation in 1532 and incidentally changed the procedure established under the Appeals Act for hearing ecclesiastical appeals. As if to emphasize the extent to which the King was taking the place of the Pope, it not only extended the prohibition of appeals to Rome to all classes of ecclesiastical suits, but provided an appeal from the Archbishop's court to the King in Chancery, to be heard by *ad hoc* commissioners nominated by the King for each case. The significance of this Act lies in the fact that it turned the surrender of ecclesiastical independence made to the King personally in 1532 into a surrender to the King in Parliament. The national representative assembly was thus both to endorse and to share in the control of the Church which the King had acquired himself two years before. The Royal Supremacy was from the beginning not a purely personal one, as is sometimes claimed, but something annexed to the Crown of England, the full powers of which were exercised only when King, Lords, and Commons acted together. Such an arrangement took away any idea of the Convocations' being legislative bodies on the same footing as Parliament, since they now had their functions and limitations defined by Act of Parliament which only parliamentary action could repeal. Though it may look so at first sight, the Henrician Reformation Settlement, which became the pattern for later ones, was not based upon the idea of the King as a quasi-ecclesiastical person, in virtue of his coronation possessing powers both in Church and State; it was a transfer of ecclesiastical authority to the State, in so far as we can think of that as distinct from the King in the sixteenth century, and the fact is only disguised from us by the much greater part played in the constitution by the personal monarchy in the sixteenth century than in later times. In Edward VI's time Bishop Gardiner recalled a conversation he had had with Lord Chancellor Audley in the previous reign. The Bishop had said that he did not see how after the establishment of the Royal Supremacy any bishop, being now a man acting under the King's authority, could be found guilty of a breach of Praemunire for interfering with secular jurisdiction. Audley replied as follows:

'Thou art a good felow, Bishop,' quod he (which was the maner of his familier speach), 'looke the Act of Supremacy, and there the King's doinges be restrayned to spiritual jurisdiction; and in a nother acte it is provided that no Spirituall Lawe shall have place contrary to a Common Lawe or Acte of Parliament. And this wer not,' quod he, 'you bishops would enter in with the Kinge and, by meanes of his supremacie, order the layty as ye listed. But we wil provide,' quod he, 'that the premunire shall ever hang over your heads, and so we lay men shalbe sure to enjoye our inheritaunce by the Common Lawes and acts of Parliament.'

So much is the Supremacy a Parliamentary one that even the King as Head of the Church statutorily cannot interfere with the King in Parliament.

The final measure to be taken was the securing of the succession, the object which had been so much in the King's mind in the whole of the divorce proceedings. The Succession Act of 1534 referred in its preface to the dangers which might ensue from an uncertain devolution of the Crown and tilted at the claims of the 'Bishop of Rome' to intervene in temporal affairs and dispose of kingdoms at his will, contrary to the divine right of kings—a topical matter, in view of the fact that Clement had threatened to depose Henry as well as to excommunicate him. It then went on to confirm Cranmer's sentence upon the King's first marriage and to declare his issue by Anne lawful heirs. The sting of the Act lay in its tail: to act or write against the succession so established was made high treason, to speak against it misprision of treason. And, in order to make cooperation in the settlement positive every subject of full age was to swear an oath to defend and observe the Act. There was doubtless no intention of carrying out the herculean task of swearing in the whole population of England, but the government was provided with a useful test it could apply to persons of importance and those thought dangerous.

No time was lost after the parliamentary session in putting the new weapon to use. Cromwell, who since the previous year had been the King's chief minister, and had advised Henry to make the breach with Rome, believed in a policy of 'Thorough'. A Renaissance statesman of the finished type, he was utterly convinced of the newer theories of sovereignty, and deterred by no scruples from putting them into effect. By his own statement he was a disciple of Machiavelli, whose *Prince* he once advised Reginald Pole to read as the epitome in political wisdom. In particular, he had fully imbibed the new conception of law as a mere command which, in virtue of the fact that it proceeded from the sovereign power, carried within itself its own justification. To the Middle Ages law had been a determination of right reason, which could be put into form by governments and enforced by them, but which they could not in the strictest sense create. To be valid, human laws had to be in accordance with that Natural Law which God imprinted in all men's reason, a reflection of that Eternal Law by which He governed the universe; and therefore laws contrary to Natural Law were null and void *ab initio* and had no claim upon men's consciences. Indeed, not only was it justifiable, in some cases it was obligatory, not to obey them. It is the difference between these two conceptions of law and political obligation which more than anything else makes the difference between the medieval world and that which followed the Renaissance, in the political sphere, and we shall see it emerging sharply in Cromwell's persecution of his and the King's opponents.

Already there had been signs of more serious opposition than the passive grumbling which had been heard in and out of Parliament, or the popular demonstrations in favour of Queen Katharine. In 1533 there had occurred the strange episode of the Nun of Kent, Elizabeth Barton. She was a woman of humble origins, who, after what was believed to be a miraculous cure from epilepsy, attained a considerable reputation for sanctity and mystical experiences. Her revelations and prophecies had attracted attention before, but it was only after the divorce question became acute that they embarrassed the government. Elizabeth took a strong line against the King's attitude and prophesied his removal within a short time if he married Anne. The failure of the prophecy gave a chance to put the Nun out of the way without loss of credit and she, with those who had encouraged her, was arrested late in 1533 and executed in April 1534 by Act of Attainder.

In itself this was no more than a minor embarrassment to Henry and his servants. But the known opinions of certain prominent men upon the royal policy induced the Crown to try to involve them in the Act of Attainder. Bishop Fisher of Rochester, Sir Thomas More, and five others were named in the Bill as guilty of misprision of treason for not revealing what they had heard from the Nun. As she had spoken to the King himself, it could hardly be claimed that the government was unaware of her statements through this alleged dereliction of duty, and the obvious aim was to frighten, and if possible punish in advance, prominent dissentients. Fisher had been in disfavour with the King since his bold defence of Katharine before the Legates, an offence which his high reputation for holiness and learning made more heinous. More, with a similar renown, had become Chancellor after

Wolsey's fall on the express understanding that he would not be expected to promote the divorce suit, to which he felt overwhelming conscientious objections. He had, however, resigned of his own volition on the day on which the Submission of the Clergy was presented to Henry—a step he had for some time wished to take. He had kept silence about the divorce question, and even consented to lay the opinions of the universities before Parliament as the constitutional spokesman for the King, without expressing his own opinion, but, as his son-in-law, Roper, says, 'doubtinge leste further attemptes after should followe, which, contrarye to his conscience, by reason of his office, he was likeleye to be put unto,' he left the administration on the plea of ill health before he could be involved in the revolution of 1533. It was particularly absurd to accuse him of complicity with Elizabeth Barton, as he had not only been doubtful of the genuineness of her gifts from the first, but had refused even to listen to reports of her prophecies about the King, and had written to warn her from meddling with such matters. Cromwell, however, suppressed evidence of More's discretion and his name was finally omitted from the Act of Attainder only after strong representations from the House of Lords. Fisher, who had not been quite so discreet and had taken the Nun's statements to be 'the threats of God', not reporting them to the King because Elizabeth had herself told them to Henry, was fined £300.

It was in the course of these proceedings that More first revealed more fully his views upon the burning topics for which he fell under suspicion, and it is interesting to examine his attitude, as that of a careful, conscientious, and moderate opponent of the King. In a letter to Cromwell of 5 March 1534 he puts into writing views he had already expressed shortly before to a commission appointed by the King to examine him. He had been urged to use this opportunity to beg their intercession that his name should be omitted from the Attainder Bill, but he told Roper afterwards that he had entirely forgotten the matter. He was evidently more anxious to discharge his conscience, for he explained his subsequent cheerfulness by saying: 'I rejoyced . . . that I had given the divill a foull fall, and that with those Lordes I had gonne so farre as without great shame I could never goe backe agayne.' He had been pressed then 'unto those thinges that the Parliament, the Bishoppes, and Universities had alreadye passed, to add his consente'—a request which indicates the value attached to his name by the King's party. He declined, pointing out that the King knew his opinion and had promised him freedom of conscience. He was then taxed with having persuaded the King to speak strongly in his book against Luther of the Pope's authority, and so exposed Henry later to a charge of inconsistency. He replied that the contrary was the case, and in his letter he explains at greater length his meaning, giving in the process a very interesting picture of his attitude to the Roman Primacy and of the development of his mind on the subject:

As touching the third point, the *primatie* of the Pope, I nothing meddle in the matter. Troth it is, that as I told you, when you desired me to shew you what I thought therein, I was my self some time not of the mind, that the primatie of that see should be begun by the institution of God, until I read in the matter those things that the Kings H. had written in his most famous book against the heretics of Martin Luther. At the first reading whereof I moved the K. H. either to leave out that point, or else to touch it more slenderly; for doubt of such things as after might hap to fal in question between his H. and some Pope: as between Princes and Popes divers times have don. Whereunto his H. answered me, that he would in no wise any thing minish of that matter . . . But surely after that I had read his G's book therein, and so many other things as I have seen in that point by this continuance of these x years since and more, have founden in effect the substance of all the holy Doctors from S. Ignatius, disciple to S. John the Evangelist, unto our own dayes, both Latins and Greeks, so consonant, and agreeing in that point, and the thing by General Councel so confirmed also, that, in good faith, I never read nor heard any thing of such effect on the other side, that ever could lead me to think, that my conscience were wel discharged, but rather in right great peril, if I should follow that other side, and deny the primatie to be provided by God. Which if we did, yet can I nothing, as I shewed you, perceive any commodity, that ever could come by that denyal. For that primatie is at the least-wise instituted by the corps of Christendome, and for a great urgent cause, in avoyding of schismes, and corroborate by continual succession more than the space of a thousand years at the least. For there are past almost a thousand years, sith the time of holy S. Gregory.

And therefore, sith al Christendom is one corps, I cannot perceive how a member thereof may, without the common assent of the body, depart from the common head. And then if we may not lawfully leave it by our selves, I cannot perceive (but if the thing were treating in a General Councel) what the question could avail, whether the primate were instituted immediately by God, or ordained by his Church? As for the General Councels assembled lawfully, I never could perceive, but that, in the declaration of the truth to be believed and to be standen to, the authority thereof ought to be taken for indubitable. Or else were there in nothing no certainty, but through Christendom, upon every mans affectionate reason, al things might be brought, fro day to day, to continual ruffle and confusion. From which by the General Councels, the Spirit of God, assisting every such Councel wel assembled, keepeth, and ever shal keep, the corps of the Catholic Church. And verily, sith the K. H. hath, as by the book of his honorable Councel appeareth, appealed to the General Councel from the Pope, (in which Councel I beseech our Lord to send his G. comfortable speed,) methinkith in my poor mind, it could be no furtherance there unto his G's cause, if his H. should in his own realm before, either by laws-making or books-putting forth, seem to derogate and deny, not only the primatie of the see apostolick, but also the authority of the General Councels. Which I verily trust his H. intendeth not. For in the next General Councel it may wel happen, that this Pope may be deposed, and another sustituted in his room, with whom the K. H. may be very well content.

For albeit that I have for mine own part such opinion of the Popes primatie, as I have shewed you, yet never thought I the Pope above the General Councel, nor never have, in any book of mine put forth among the Kings subjects in our vulgar tongue, avaunced greatly the Popes authority . . .

More's opinions on the Papacy, then, though they had developed, ironically enough through Henry's own theological arguments, were what would later be termed Gallican. His chief concern is for the unity of the Church and he is opposing that national particularism in religion which Henry and Cromwell were busy in establishing. There comes out too that contemporary reverence for royalty which made More say as little as he could in public against the King's policies. He explains at length what pains he had taken to see the King's side in the divorce suit, even to the extent of refusing to read the arguments against it. He had the sixteenth-century idea of the duties of a royal servant. He did all he could by reading and conference to see the King's case.

After this did I nothing more therin; nor never any word wrot I therin, to the impairing of his G's part, neither before nor after, nor any man ellys by my procurement: but settling my mind in quiet to serve his G. in other things, I would not so much as look, nor wittingly let ly by me any book of the other part. Albeit that I gladly read afterwards divers books that were made on his part yet.

More, then, was no active counter-revolutionary. Yet he was regarded as dangerous, and when in April he refused the oath required by the Succession Act, he was committed to the Tower. He was willing, he explained, to swear to observe the succession, but the oath (not prescribed in detail in the statute but apparently composed later) required those to whom it was administered both to swear to the observance of the other statutes which abolished papal authority and, by its demand that the taker should swear allegiance 'alonely to the King's majesty . . . and not to any other within this Realm, nor foreign authority', also implied renunciation of the Pope. To Cranmer's ingenious suggestion that obedience to the King was a more immediate clear duty than his doubt whether he could conscientiously take the oath (for More had said that he did not condemn the consciences of those that had sworn) he replied ironically that the argument was a simple way out of perplexities. 'For in whatsoever matter the doctours stand in gret doubt, the kinges commaundement given upon whither side he list, foyleth all the doutes.' To the assertion that he ought to 'change' his conscience to conform with that of the Great Council of the Realm he replied:

If there were no mo but my selfe upon my side, and the whole parlement upon the tother, I woulde be sore afraid to leane to my owne minde againste so many. But on the other side, if it so be, that in some thinges for which I refuse the othe, I have as I thinke I have, upon my part as great a counsail and a greater to, I am not than bounden to change my consciens, and conforme it to the counsail of one realme against the general counsaile of Christendome.

He was, as always, standing out for the medieval belief in a supra-national Christian community, to which his first allegiance was due.

With him to the Tower went Fisher, who had also refused the oath. Recalcitrance like theirs was rare. All over the country clergy, prominent laity, and members of the religious orders were accepting the new regime. The only notable refusals were by members of the reformed or unrelaxed religious orders, the Observant Franciscans and the Carthusians, some of whom were later to suffer with the two more prominent martyrs. But there were troubles of another sort to keep the Government anxious. There was always the risk of an invasion by Charles V, to which his ambassador was constantly urging him with statements that England would rise to help him. Chapuys could report that many of the great northern and western lords were in treasonable correspondence with him, and even some of those of the less turbulent south-east. As a foreigner he probably overestimated the support which a rising in aid of a foreign invasion would gain. But there was also the possibility of Scottish help, whilst in Ireland the Earl of Kildare was already in rebellion and had openly declared for Pope and Emperor. Moreover there was a candidate to the throne ready to hand. The weakness of the Tudor claim to the throne, judged by legitimist principles, could always be Henry's Achilles heel. The Poles, descended from George, Duke of Clarence, Edward IV's brother, could be regarded as more certain heirs of the Plantagenets than the reigning dynasty, whose hereditary claims were derived from the originally illegitimate Beauforts and a daughter of Edward IV only. Reginald Pole, though a younger son, had taken refuge abroad since 1529 as a result of his refusal to lend himself to the divorce plan; every effort had been made to gain one who was a scholar of distinction as well as a man of note in the aristocracy, but he had declined to be won and was in 1536 to write his *De Unitate Ecclesiae* against Henry's schism. He was already being suggested as a pretender whom the Emperor could back and later there were ideas of marrying him to the Princess Mary.

All, however, came to nothing. Charles never moved and Henry probably owed his safety largely to the loyalty of his discarded wife, who, in spite of indignities, attempts to make her admit the lawfulness of the sentence against her, and separation from her daughter, would never lend herself to plots against the man she still regarded as husband. So the King and Cromwell could go on with the process of consolidating their work. There were a few loose ends to be gathered up before the new theory of Church and State could be regarded as complete. In March of 1534 the Convocation of Canterbury, to be followed in May by that of York, had replied negatively to the question 'Whether the Roman pontiff has any greater jurisdiction conferred on him by God in Holy Scripture, within this realm of England, than any other foreign bishop', and this doctrinal decision was backed up by intensive propaganda from pulpit and press. In November the Act of Supremacy formally confirmed the King's right to be 'taken accepted and reputed the only supreme Head in earth of the Church of England', with the explanation that this gave him full power of visitation of ecclesiastical bodies, together with the right of reforming and punishing all ecclesiastical offences, thus transferring to him the papal administrative rights in England. Another Succession Act reinforced the former, and the Annates, which had been such a grievance when paid to Rome, were now granted to the King. At the same time a measure destined to be used against those who were refusing to swear to the new arrangements was passed. The Treasons Act, for the first time in English history, made words high treason, by enacting that anyone who attempted to deprive the King, Queen, or their heirs of 'their dignity title or name of their royal estates' was a traitor. This of course implied that to deny the Royal Supremacy, which was now part of the King's title, was punishable. The bill not unnaturally met with great opposition during its passage, and the objectors managed to get the word 'maliciously' inserted in the definition of the newly created treason, with the idea of ensuring that mere idle words should not incur the death penalty. But, as the Act was used by Cromwell, this was to prove a vain precaution.

The year 1535 saw the carrying into effect of the measures thus devised against prominent resisters of the King's will. Fisher and More had already been attainted of misprision of treason and deprived of their property. Now they were to suffer the utmost penalty of the law. A foretaste of the method to be adopted was to be seen in the case of the recalcitrant Carthusians, who in April were first forced to incriminate themselves, by being asked whether they would obey Henry as Head of the English Church, and then condemned for treason under the new Act, the judges apparently laying down that anyone who denied the Royal Supremacy necessarily did so maliciously. In June both the Bishop and the ex-Lord Chancellor, having been tricked into making statements to royal officials which could be regarded as denials of the Supremacy, were found guilty of treason. More denied even the correctness of the words reported against him by Rich, the Solicitor-General, and used all his legal ability to argue the invalidity of his conviction; but it availed nothing. Fisher was beheaded on 22 June and More on 6 July.

The executions were a sign that Henry would stop at nothing. As More himself had said, when advising Cromwell, in counselling the King, always to tell him what he ought to do and never what he was able to do, 'For yf the lyone knewe his owne strengthe, harde were it for any man to rule him'. The lion had tasted absolute power and the appetite came in eating. To execute in one year both the one English bishop regarded as a saint, and the one layman of the realm who bore a famous and untarnished European reputation, argued an indifference to the opinion of Christendom which showed the degree to which Henry had broken with the very idea of a world Christian community. It was to that world community that More had made his appeal. After conviction, when he could speak his mind freely in open court, he gave his grounds for believing that the verdict was morally untenable:

Forasmuch, my lorde, quothe he, as this inditement is grounded uppon an Acte of Parliament directly repugnant to the lawes of God and His Holy Churche, the supreme governement of which, or of any parte wherof, may noe temperall prince presume by any lawe to take uppon him, as rightfully belonginge to the Sea of Roome, a spirituall prehemynencye by the mouthe of our Saviour Himselfe, personally present uppon the earth, only to St. Peter and his successors, Bishoppes of the same Sea, by speciall prerogatyve granted; it is therefore in lawe, amongst christian men, insufficient to chardge any Christyan man. And for profe thereof, as amonge divers other reasons and auctorityes, he declared that like as this realme, beinge but one member and small part of the Churche, might not make a particular lawe disagreeinge with the generall lawe of Christes Universall Catholike Churche, noe more then the Citty of London, beinge but one poore member in respecte of the whole realme, might make a law agaynst an Acte of Parliament to bynde the whole realme.

In that speech was succinctly expressed the assumptions upon which England had lived since her conversion to Christianity. More took for granted both the limited nature of national sovereignty and the conception of law as something which could have reality only if it was conformed to the eternal order of things. He was opposing the doctrines of the omnicompetent, irresponsible state, and of law as the mere expression of power. If he died a martyr for the Pope, he died also for these conceptions of political philosophy.

6

Disendowment and Reaction

THE ESSENTIAL CRISIS of Henry VIII's reign ended with
the passing of the laws establishing the Royal Supremacy and
the terrorizing of gainsayers by the relatively few dramatic
executions. The moment for counter-revolution to strike
was then, and, when reaction by force came, it was too late
and too partial to have much hope of success. It is significant
of the attitude of the ordinary Englishman that it was not
until the first changes were made in the apparatus of everyday
religion that this point was reached. It was the dissolution
of the monasteries which brought about the first and only
large-scale rising which Henry VIII had to meet, and even
that was limited to that part of the country in which the
monastic life was still most intimately bound up with the
popular faith. The sixteenth-century Englishman had inherited Catholicism as a traditional practice rather than as a
completely understood theory; royal marriage cases and their
canonical complications were above his head and so was the
question in what sense the King could be Head of the Church.
He might and did grumble at the King's putting away of a
popular Queen, and in many cases he probably disliked this
new idea of a lay Pope. But neither of these things affected
anything but the preaching in his parish church and, as
Gardiner was later to affirm, 'it is contrary to the inclination
of us Englishmen to be long in the state of hearers'. What
Gardiner said of the situation in 1547 was doubtless true
earlier: 'Such as be most rude are led to good life by imitation

rather than hearing. They move in the body of the church in much simplicity; and when they have heard words spoken in the pulpit they report they were good and very good and wondrous good . . . but what they were . . . they cannot tell.' So it is doubtful whether the many sermons commanded to be preached against the Pope and in support of the King's Supremacy had as much effect as the government expected, whether for good or ill.

It was not to be quite the same when that government began to change what had been for centuries a prominent feature of town and countryside, the abbeys, priories, and friaries.

Of the motives for the dissolution much has been written, but it would seem that a simple explanation covers nearly all the facts: it was a financial measure. The researches of Dietz have made plain how desperate was the King's need for money. The accumulation of treasure brought about by Henry VII's careful management of the royal estates, and other permanent sources of revenue, and his parsimony and skill in extracting extra taxation had been dissipated by the exuberant expenditure of his young son and Wolsey in foreign adventures and display in the earlier part of the reign. Now the coffers were empty and the seizure of the wealth of the monasteries was the most easily defensible measure of confiscation of church property, and the one least likely to rouse resistance. There was already small-scale precedent for it, and it would not affect directly a large class of the community, in the way that an attack upon chantries or parish endowments would have done. There is every reason to think that this was the chief object in view, and it was probably this measure which was in Cromwell's mind when he told Henry, as it is said, that he could make him the richest king in Christendom.

It is a mistake to imagine that the putting down of the monks was a necessary corollary of the abolition of Papal jurisdiction. There is no evidence to show that the religious, except in a small number of cases, were any more papally minded than other people in England. With the few exceptions already noted, the monks and friars accepted the Royal Supremacy without demur and signed documents to say so; some were even to boast to Cromwell of their zeal against the Bishop of Rome's usurpations. The idea that the policy of dissolution was dictated by the desire to remove scandals, or to increase the efficiency of the Church by doing away with an effete part of its structure, has even less to commend it; it is contradicted by the testimonial to the good state of some larger monasteries given in the Act for the suppression of the smaller ones. If in some 'great solemn monasteries' 'religion was right well kept and observed', why were they in turn suppressed in the course of the next few years? And can it be believed that the line of demarcation between good and corrupt houses accurately followed that between those of £200 a year revenues and those of less, as the Act might appear to suggest? Monastic scandals were good propaganda, but the cynical way in which this propaganda was handled makes it impossible that this can have been the real motive of the government, just as the relatively small proportion of the confiscated property actually expended upon new bishoprics rules out of court the claim that the object was the better redistribution of church property. Cromwell was the last man in the world to be seriously worried about monastic morals, or about the best use of ecclesiastical endowments; as a Machiavellian he held a low view of human nature at best, and as a realist statesman he considered that the best possible use of church lands was to enrich the King and his supporters. With the utmost charity we cannot but attribute the lowest motives to those who destroyed the religious houses; to do otherwise would be historical wishful thinking of the most naïve type.

To say this, however, is not to say that English sixteenth-century monasticism was beyond reproach, or that there was not a real case for a reform which would have involved a great diminution in the number of its foundations. The best evidence of this is the fact that such ideas were entertained at the time by men of unimpeachable Catholic orthodoxy. The often quoted *Consilium de emendanda Ecclesia*, drawn up in 1538 by a committee, on which Cardinal Pole served, to advise the Pope on measures of reform, recommended the gradual abolition of conventual mendicants by the prohibition of new professions of novices, on the ground that the orders were a scandal to the laity and set a bad example to the world. To reform them back to their original zeal was considered impossible. And in England precedents for suppression had been set, not only by the worldly Wolsey, who got rid of no less than twenty-one houses to endow his new foundation of Cardinal College, Oxford (the later Christ Church, itself on the site of the suppressed Priory of St. Frideswide), and his school at Ipswich, but also by the saintly and orthodox Fisher and by Bishop Alcock of Ely, who founded Jesus College, Cambridge, out of the buildings and revenues of a nunnery. There was even an expectation of a coming general suppression or disappearance of monasticism, together with a doubt of the usefulness of monks, among some Englishmen who had no sympathy with heresy. Bishop Oldham, founder of Manchester Grammar School, wrote to Bishop Fox of Winchester to dissuade him from attaching his new college of Corpus Christi at Oxford to a monastery:

What, my lord, shall we build houses and provide livelihood for a company of bussing monks, whose end and fall we may live to see; no, no, it is more mete a great deal that we should have care to provide for the increase of learning, and for such as who by their learning, shall do good in the church and commonwealth.

But here again exaggeration must be avoided. The widespread idea that the religious orders had lost all their popularity in England and were generally despised is not borne out by the evidence. As Janelle has shown, legacies to the religious orders continued to be frequent, though one can trace some discrimination in those so favoured. The great Northern Cistercian houses, later to be championed by the Pilgrimage of Grace, and the relatively poor friars (poor by the evidence of their goods seized at the Dissolution) profited more than others, whilst the reformed Observant Franciscans and the unrelaxed Carthusian ascetics can be shown to have had greater spiritual influence in London than other religious.

The inference sometimes made from the cessation of new religious foundations in the later Middle Ages—only three in the whole of the fifteenth century—that monasticism was regarded as obsolete, has been made without due consideration of the fact that there must come a saturation point in such matters and that England possessed by the fourteenth century all the houses which could be kept in being by the recruits supplied from her almost stationary population. As has been shown, the houses founded earlier, comparatively few of which had ceased to exist, did not lack gifts up to the last.

On the other hand a different story is told by the emptiness of many monasteries as revealed in the periodical visitations. (This was not as great as used to be believed. The heavy losses in the Black Death were partly made up by a rapid recovery up to about 1420, after which the increase was slower. By 1500 numbers stood just below 75 per cent of the peak reached about 1300.) This was at least one cause of the slackness, financial mismanagement, and general air of decay, to which again the visitations often witness. A few monks living in a house designed for greater numbers would have considerable excuse for disheartenment and might easily grow slack. Worse still, by no means all the inhabitants of the religious houses had any true vocation to their life, as is witnessed by the appeals of some monks to Cromwell's visitors to be allowed to leave, the frequent references in visitation reports to 'apostates' who had run away, and the subsequent careers of most of those expelled in the Dissolution. Baskerville showed how few went overseas or made any attempt to continue the life to which they had originally dedicated themselves. The majority, having accepted the Government's pensions, tried if possible to obtain posts as secular clergymen, and a large proportion were successful; some of these later married, and one can trace cases of ex-religious retaining benefices until old age, having conformed to the kaleidoscopic religious changes of the period between Henry VIII and Elizabeth. There can have been little enthusiasm for the religious life among the majority of sixteenth-century English religious.

This fact is to be explained to a great extent by the wae in which the monasteries had been recruited in the Middle Ages. The element of personal choice was in some cases minimal. The clothing of novices as young as fifteen seems to have been not unusual in the fifteenth century, despite rules fixing a riper age. Nor was release from the obligation of the religious life easy for those who had entered it in the rashness of youth or been enticed or forced into it by parents or others. This explains the laxity, formal observance, or actual misbehaviour which the visitations show us; the old principle of the Benedictine Rule, by which it was much easier to get out of a monastery than to get in, had been forgotten, both in houses which followed it and elsewhere.

How far immorality and crime were widespread in the monasteries is a question which has unfortunately become a field of controversy between those whose historical eyes have been too much influenced by theological considerations. No one now takes the *Comperta* of Cromwell's visitors, with their highly coloured and often salacious accusations, at their face value; they were from the beginning intended to be propaganda to support a policy already decided upon, and often the hearsay, if not fictional, character of some of the evidence is apparent by inspection. Moreover their statements are sometimes contradicted by the evidence of the royal commissioners, largely local men, who actually carried out the suppressions which followed. But it would be foolish therefore to suppose that all monasteries were nurseries of sanctity, or even respectable. The evidence of visitation returns of the period before the Dissolution, made by bishops who had no interest in denigrating the monks, shows many scandals, often of long continuance, which can hardly have disappeared by the time the King's hand fell. One must allow something for the medieval character, simple and extreme both in sanctity and in sin; there was not the worship then of outward respectability which in later times was to preserve many from blatant vice from no higher motive than fear of public loss of face. One must allow too for the general decay of morality which is such a feature of the later

Middle Ages and sixteenth century: the monks were no worse than their neighbours in the world and probably rather better. Yet, if one remembers the essential conception of the religious life as one of stricter self-devotion than was possible in the world, it will be seen how very paradoxical it is for such a defence to be possible.

Nor was it the breaches of the vow of chastity or the anger and bitterness, leading even to physical violence, which not infrequently occurred, nor the stealing and fraud practised by some monks upon their fellows, which were the most deadly symptoms of decay. Much more symptomatic, because more inveterate and habitual, was the laxity of observance, the half-heartedness about the worship and contemplation which formed the *raison d'être* of the religious life. Few English monks can have asked St. Bernard's constant question to himself, *Ad quid venisti*? They had slipped into a barely comprehended, and rarely examined, routine, the observances of which were often evaded, and more often performed unwillingly or half-heartedly. The sixteenth-century monastic houses have been well compared with eighteenth-century Oxford and Cambridge colleges; there is the same forgetfulness of purpose, the same unenlightened clinging to the husks of tradition, and the same evasion of duty, varied by a good deal of more or less scandalous conduct and vice. Just as there were energetic and able scholars to be found in the universities before the nineteenth-century reforms, so there were saints still to be discovered in sixteenth-century monasteries; but in both cases they were a minority and the average varied from the lukewarm to the scandalous and vicious. Such would seem a reasonable judgement on the evidence available.

Of the services of the monasteries to the world there is much the same to be said. Some communities, like the Carthusians, as has been pointed out, were real spiritual guides to those who resorted to their churches and confessionals, but for the most part not much aid of the kind the monks should have been peculiarly able to give came from them, and in some cases they merely set bad examples, or, by selfish use of their privileges, aroused hatred. Learning had long ceased to be a monastic monopoly, and indeed not a few monks were almost illiterate, though Canterbury Cathedral Priory, for example, under Prior Selling was a home of the revived classical studies. Contrary to popular belief, the monasteries were never in the Middle Ages schools for any but their inmates; general teaching was the province of the cathedral schools, universities, and town grammar schools. Monasteries had been the great centres of manuscript production and of historical writing, but both activities had largely ceased by this time. The monastic chronicler was being replaced by the municipal or private chronicler, and too often the monks had their books written for them by scriveners at a price. The wealth of the orders had increasingly induced them to buy the services which according to the original ideal they should have carried out for themselves; servants of one kind or another tended to be as numerous as monks within abbey walls, if not more so. Manual work, no less than intellectual, had become a rarity in monastic life, and, apart from maintaining the round of services (which even so was sometimes carried out upon a rota system), the monk was too often inclined to remain in inglorious idleness with, in many cases, the proverbial result. Nor was abbey almsgiving such a potent force in preventing destitution as it has been sometimes represented. We are perhaps less inclined than our ancestors to be shocked, on the principles of the Gradgrind philosophy, by its indiscriminate character, which was perhaps its most Christian feature; but the real criticism of it is that it was not plentiful enough. Savine calculated that not more than 3 per cent of monastic revenues was spent in this way just before the Dissolution. It was not merely the disappearance of the monasteries which created the later sixteenth-century problem of poverty and its concomitant, the unimaginative and savage Tudor Poor Law—though the character of that law may have owed something to the disappearance of the visible witness to the unstrained character of Christian mercy which the monasteries provided even in their most decadent days. Sixteenth-century poverty was the result of the social and economic upheaval which was destroying medieval society, and which coincided with the end of the monasteries.

It was, then, a dusty and creaking system, shabby in decay, which was now to be swept away. It could no doubt have rejuvenated itself, as Continental parallels show; but it was not to be given the chance. The process of dissolution was accomplished by the use of the visitatorial powers conferred upon the Crown by the Supremacy Act of 1534. Cromwell had been named the King's deputy or 'Vicar General' for this purpose in January 1535, and in July he began visitations by his own deputies in the monastic houses on the traditional pattern hitherto used by bishops or papal delegates. By next year the reports were available. Their character has been already mentioned; it was to be expected from the men who were chosen as visitors, of whom no one has been able to say better than that they were not as bad as they have sometimes been made out to be. Cromwell had a genius for finding birds of his own feather. It was on their evidence that the Act of February 1536, suppressing the smaller religious houses, was made law, though not without difficulty —if later stories are to be believed, by threats from the King himself. The actual work of closure and confiscation was begun that spring by local commissioners; the property was handed over to the new Court of Augmentations to administer for the King, and the religious given the option of going to the larger houses still to remain, or, if in Orders, accepting 'capacities' or licences to serve as secular clergymen. A large number—perhaps more than half—seem to have chosen the latter course, which is another indication of the waning of the monastic spirit. Those who moved elsewhere to continue their vocation, however, could not keep to their choice for long. By 1537 the larger houses began to fall, mainly by individual surrenders technically voluntary. In 1539 a Bill was passed to confirm these surrenders and by March 1540 the whole affair was finished with the surrender of Waltham Abbey. The hollowness of the distinction drawn in 1536 between the great and small houses in virtue and observance was thereby exposed, for it can hardly be doubted that the real motive was merely to secure all monastic property, once the first experiment had proved its benefit to the State. But it must also be remembered that between these years had occurred the one and only armed rebellion against Henrician policy, and that directly as a result of the attack upon the monasteries. So the alarmed government, both in revenge, and to take away as rapidly as possible any remains of the old state of things which another counter-revolutionary rising could try to defend, made a clean sweep.

The Pilgrimage of Grace, which began after local disturbances in Lincolnshire in October 1536 and spread to the greater part of northern England, was broken up at the end of the year by the promise of concessions and stamped out, by military force and a series of executions and other punishments, in the earlier part of 1537. It was an interesting and pathetic movement, both for its revelation of how deeply the principle of submission to authority had entered even into the minds of turbulent North-countrymen, so that they were more willing to parley with than to fight the King, and for its varied causes. That its primary motive was discontent with the religious changes already effected and fear of those to come, need not be doubted. The Lincolnshire rising was inspired partly by rumours that parish churches would be plundered by the King, as monasteries had already been. Further north, when a more or less organized army was formed, this marched with religious emblems and described its purpose as a Pilgrimage. But there were other factors at work as well. The North, besides being conservative in religion, was conservative politically, and disliked the Tudor policy of centralization and the destruction of the old feudal franchises, which kept their vitality longest in this remote and economically undeveloped part of England. Its people did not wish to be governed exclusively from London. This comes out, not only in their complaints of the King's advisers, whom they suspected of heretical tendencies and thought were going to push religious changes even further than they had already gone, but in their demands for a Parliament to be held 'at Nottingham or York, and that shortly', for the re-enfranchisement of Yorkshire boroughs which had lost Parliamentary representation and for local men, and not 'king's servants', to sit in the House of Commons. The nobles among them resented the new Statute of Uses, by which they ceased to escape the payments due to the King for much of their land; the poorer men wanted the recognition of tenant right and the putting into force of the statutes against enclosures. All alike resented taxation and the fact that its proceeds were not used for local purposes. In ecclesiastical matters they wanted a cessation of monastic dissolutions and the restoration of the abbeys already put down. (The great abbeys of the North both provided hospitality in bleak country and helped their poor neighbours by alms.) They demanded the suppression of heresy. About the Royal Supremacy they were less decided: the original rebels in Lincolnshire were ready to accept it, and now its abolition was asked for only in so far as it touched the cure of souls, the supreme power in which matter ought to be left, they held, to the See of Rome. They were agreeable to some limitations on the Pope's powers and exactions in England—the abolition of Annates for example. They wanted Princess Mary declared legitimate by Act of Parliament, chiefly, they alleged, in order to avoid a Scottish succession, James V of Scotland being Henry's nearest male relative—a very comprehensible motive in the traditionally anti-Scottish North. There is little in all this of abstract theory: the grievances of the Pilgrims were practical ones, and they wanted the pattern of religion and social life with which they had been familiar for centuries preserved to them without adulteration by new-fangled, South-country ways. It was the voice of the most traditional part of Old England speaking, almost for the last time.

Henry's responses betrayed again and again his anger at any questioning of his right to do as he pleased. What shocked and annoyed him most was the very fact of resistance at all, 'your shameful insurrection and unnatural rebellion', as he called it. He disliked the idea of parley with the rebels and had to be mollified by the undertaking of the Duke of Norfolk, his general, that he would not observe any promises he might have to make to the insurgents. However, the military situation made temporizing necessary, and the Pilgrimage was persuaded to disperse on promise of pardon and redress of grievances. Suspicion between the lords who had led the movement and the commons who had followed them was roused by doubts as to whether the Government would really satisfy their demands, and a revival of disorders gave an excuse for the King to turn to a policy of repression and to stamp out the rising with a long series of executions. The crisis was over without Henry's having had to retrace any steps of his new order.

Still, it had been an awkward moment. The rising was too local, too far from the centre of government, to have much chance of seizing power, and the rebels were far too fundamentally law-abiding to carry through a successful counter-revolution. They had sedulously avoided attacking the King in person and attributed all their woes to his advisers; the royal herald sent to read a proclamation to them found the rank and file giving 'great honour to the king's coat of arms'. They seem to have had no thought of changing the dynasty and shouted for no pretender. Nor did they even angle for foreign support. The Pope, on hearing of the disturbance, sent Reginald Pole as his Legate to Flanders to organize support for it. Not only did he arrive too late, but there was never any disposition in the North to seek his help. The sentiment of almost unreasoning loyalty to an established King, as a religious and moral duty, was strong enough even in the turbulent North to prevent a recourse to extreme measures. The doctrine of the Divine Right of Kings, in a non-legitimist form, was gaining ground. It was always to be the chief strength of the English monarchy throughout the Reformation.

Nevertheless one can trace a modification of policy partly to the shock given by the Pilgrimage of Grace. Henceforward the pace of change was to be slower, and at times there was to be reaction. Other events had paved the way for this. In particular Anne Boleyn was out of the way. Henry's infatuation for her waned when she failed to produce a male heir. Once again Henry believed that the curse of God was upon him, that his second marriage was the result of witchcraft and must also be null and void. In the spring of 1536 she was sent to the Tower on charges of immoral conduct, and beheaded within a month. Whether guilty or not, she ceased to be a factor in the situation, and, as Katharine of Aragon had died at the beginning of the year, the King was for the first time free, on any theory, to marry whom he would. The succession question, however, was as difficult as ever, since, before Anne's death, Cranmer had declared the Boleyn marriage null *ab initio*, most probably on the ground of Henry's previous relations with her sister, Mary Boleyn, which had created an impediment to it. The fact had been well known at the time of the wedding, and, when negotiating for his divorce from Katharine of Aragon, the King had obtained from the Pope an advance dispensation, so that, once he was free, Anne could be his wife. But consistency was never his strong point and he had now bastardized his second daughter, as well as his first.

All this had incidentally strengthened England's position in foreign affairs, for now there was no continuing ground for quarrel with Charles V. That, in turn, meant that Henry could cease to flirt for an alliance with Charles's Protestant subjects, the disaffected princes of the Empire, who had been an assurance against united Imperial action against him. He never had much affection for Lutherans, useful as they might be on occasion, and could never be persuaded to make common cause with them against Rome. In 1534 he had opened negotiations, in which he used Barnes, the English Lutheran (whom he was afterwards to burn as a heretic), and was invited to join the Evangelical League of Princes. But both the League's monetary demands, and their stickling for adherence to the Augsburg Confession of Lutheran doctrine, proved obstacles, and nothing effective had been done by the time of Anne Boleyn's death. The news of this was received with dismay in Lutheran circles, which knew the connexions of the Boleyn party with the Reformers, but the execution did not in fact radically alter English policy. Cromwell remained in favour. Henry immediately married Jane Seymour in a new, and as it happened, successful attempt to provide a male heir, and, so far from seeking reconciliation with Rome, had a new Act of Parliament passed in the summer, which made supports of Papal authority liable to the penalties of Praemunire and styled the Papal Supremacy a wresting of God's word 'excluding Christ out of his kingdom and rule of man's soul'. The Convocation, which as usual accompanied the Parliament, set out the Ten Articles which, more by omission than by positive statement, attempted to make an accommodation with Lutheran theology in the light of the negotiations which had been going on with the Wittenberg theologians. Officially they were designed to put an end to the disputes about doctrine which were raging in the country, of which the clergy had complained. But there can be little doubt that they were also designed to meet the desires of the Lutherans as far as possible; in the Wittenberg Articles of this year the latter had gone as far as they could in conciliating the more traditional outlook of the English, and the influence of these upon the Ten Articles is obvious. The Ten Articles mentioned only three sacraments, without notice of the traditional four others but without denying them. They phrased the teaching upon the Real Presence in such a way that the definition was compatible with either transubstantiation or the Lutheran doctrine of 'impanation'. On the vital point of justification they made affirmations without attacking any particular point of view, and they spoke of the old Catholic practices of honouring images, praying to saints, and using certain ceremonies, in such a way as, without forbidding them, to acknowledge that there had been superstitions in connexion with them. They commended prayers for the dead, but declared that 'the place where they be, the name thereof, and kind of pains there . . . be to us uncertain by scripture', thereby leaving undefined the doctrine of Purgatory. They were in fact the first of the ingeniously ambiguous documents which were so often to be used to maintain a degree of unity in the various stages of the English Reformation. So long as Cromwell remained in power hopes of an alliance with the German Lutherans were never abandoned.

His fall, despite the Pilgrimage of Grace, did not take place until 1540, and was not in itself responsible for the reaction to a more medieval attitude towards doctrine and practice which becomes apparent from 1539. We are in fact already passing into the period, which extends until the end of the reign, in which two parties, Protestant and Henrician Conservative (i.e., those who accepted the Royal Supremacy, but wished to retain Catholic doctrine and practice), struggle for influence, the King holding the balance between them and using each for his own purposes. Cromwell, Cranmer, and Latimer represent the first, Gardiner and the Duke of Norfolk the second. From 1537 to 1539 the Reformers on the whole had the better of it. The suppression of monasteries continued and, with the granting of their lands to friends and supporters of the King, a group was being built up with a strong financial interest in the maintenance of the disendowment policy, a group consisting not only of the original buyers, but also of those who had bought or leased land from them. Mary's reign was to show how potent an influence this was against the re-establishment of the medieval system. (It must be noticed that it was not only those of Protestant sympathies who received the lands: the Duke of Norfolk for example was one of the largest grantees.) In doctrine, the period is noteworthy for the *Bishops' Book* of 1537, which represents a swing away from the tacit unorthodoxy of the Ten Articles. It seems to have originated in a dispute between the two parties in the episcopate. In giving definitions of the four sacraments omitted in 1536, it filled what the conservatives considered a gap in the exposition of the Faith. It gave at great length the reasons for rejecting papal authority and the view of the Church's nature resulting therefrom, but there was no positive denial of Lutheran notions, and it is to be noticed that both schools of thought among the clergy signed it, which, even making allowance for the fact that to refuse to do so would have incurred the King's anger, suggests that those who see in it elements of compromise are right.

In 1538 the continuing flirtation with the German Lutherans brought about the visit of a delegation of Lutheran divines to England for conference. From it emerged thirteen articles on which agreement was reached, though on other points the negotiators had merely to agree to differ. No official athuority was ever given to the thirteen decisions, which were really no more than a stage in a religio-political alliance never finally concluded. Indeed the English fishing for Continental allies now took a more dynastic and less theological turn; it was to the less rigid of the Lutheran princes that Henry now turned, instead of to the Schmalkaldic League, and the project of an alliance crystallized into the famous match with Anne of Cleves, daughter of the Duke of Cleves. Jane Seymour's death in giving birth to the future Edward VI made Henry a possible, if scarcely eligible, *parti* once again, and Cromwell, to his own ultimate ruin, pressed through the marriage with Anne, which took place early in 1540. Its immediate failure—for Henry had taken a distaste for the lady at first sight, so he later asserted—was followed by Cromwell's fall and execution that same summer, perhaps not so much for this reason as from a reaction on the King's part against the whole policy of alliance with the Reformation which the minister had tried to pursue. Henry, as the Lutherans saw, had never had any enthusiasm for the Gospel as they understood it; the 'Gospel according to Harry', they asserted, was the wealth of the Church. That gained he would probably much have preferred, either an independent position as virtual Pope of a national Catholic Church, or an accommodation on his own terms with Rome, arranged by the pressure of Catholic Continental allies. This policy seems best to explain the reaction against Protestantism which began very obviously in 1539 and only culminated next year in the dropping of Cromwell. The spring Parliament of the former year was recommended by the King to consider the suppression of diversity in religion. The outcome of this was the Act of Six Articles, in which the King is reported to have had a great personal share. By it the denial of six points of traditional belief and practice—transubstantiation, the sufficiency of communion in one kind, clerical celibacy, the binding force of vows of chastity, the rightfulness of private Masses, and the necessity of auricular confession—was made penal. It is significant that some of these were points which had made theological agreement with the Lutherans impossible. Though the new policy thus inaugurated was as Erastian as before, since the proceedings took place in Parliament, not Convocation, and was carried largely by the influence of the laity, who, wrote one of them, were 'all of one opinion', the Royal Supremacy was henceforth to be used in a conservative direction.

Yet, even so, the expected stamping out of new opinions, which Protestants abroad feared on the first receipt of the news, did not take place, and Henry continued to the end of his reign to be to some extent a Mr. Facing-both-ways. Barnes, one of the most prominent English Lutherans, who had earlier been used in the negotiations with Wittenberg, was burned with others in July 1540, two days after Cromwell was beheaded. But there was never a complete purge, and, most significant of all, Protestant influences were not excluded from the episcopal bench. Latimer and Shaxton resigned their sees and were for a time imprisoned; but Cranmer remained Archbishop and Henry steadfastly resisted and checkmated the repeated efforts of his enemies to unseat him. To the end of the reign the reforming Archbishop retained his King's confidence, and it was his hand which the dying Henry pressed upon his deathbed as an assurance of his faith in Christ. The history of the last six and a half years of Henry VIII indeed is that of an administration balanced between the Old Learning and the New, as the contemporary phraseology would have put it, with policy determined by a powerful and incalculable King who knew how to use men of differing opinions as an effective, if sometimes unwilling, team. How far Henry, had he lived longer, might have gone in the direction of Protestantism it is difficult to say. Though the last doctrinal formulary of the reign, the so-called *King's Book* of 1543, was outwardly severely Catholic, it still contained language which derived ultimately from Luther and had been preserved from the *Bishops' Book* of 1537, which in turn had borrowed it from an English Primer of the period just after the breach with Rome, and at certain points it was less than explicit on the Catholic side of controverted questions. As a recent author has said, 'there is enough compromise in the shaping of the King's Book to have enabled the Reformers to hope that the Word of God had not lost the upper hand'. Projects of liturgical reform too were prepared by Cranmer and discussed by Convocation; in 1545 an English Litany, which severely cut down the older series of addresses to the saints, was authorized for use. After Henry's death Cranmer, normally a trustful man, asserted that in 1546 he himself had been astonished at the King's forwardness in the cause of reform. There was, it seems, a project for an alliance with Francis I of France, by which 'the king's majesty and the French king had been at this point, not only within half a year after to have changed the mass into a communion, as we now use it, but also utterly to have extirpated and banished the bishop of Rome and his usurped power out of both their realms and dominions', and they planned too to invite Charles V to join them. Those who hold that Henry remained an anti-Protestant to the end have also to explain the singular fact that the heir to the throne, Prince Edward, was educated by uniformly Protestant tutors, even his French instructor, John Balmaine, being a heretic by the standards of his own country.

On the other hand, indications are not wanting even of feelers for a rapprochement with the Pope. In 1541 Gardiner, when on an embassy to the Emperor, listened to proposals of this kind and the Duke of Norfolk, whose attainder just preceded Henry's death, was alleged to have been plotting a restoration of papal supremacy. Gardiner later asserted that on more than one occasion after the schism Henry had mediated a reconciliation, and it may well be that he was not always deaf to advice in this direction. Indeed his personal views about religion, no less than his policy, remain an enigma and he probably had not a little of the versatility of his daughter Elizabeth. Like her he strove for national unity in religion; in his last speech to Parliament he rebuked both those who were 'too stiff in their old Mumpsimus' and those who were 'too busy and curious in their new Sumpsimus', and announced, 'There is one thing to which I require you, and that is charity and concord.' To this, and to the exigences of foreign policy, religion was made subservient, and indeed, if a key to his apparent vagaries is to be sought, it must be looked for here. It is significant to notice how the ebb and flow of religious innovation corresponds to the variations of Continental affairs and to England's position in relation to them. In 1545 Cranmer's proposals for the abolition of some old ceremonies seem to have been defeated by representations from Gardiner, who was endeavouring to conclude a league with both France and the Empire, that further changes in religion would alienate Continental sympathy. The ultimate motives of Henry's proceedings are perhaps not ill judged in a letter of the exiled Protestant, Hooper, at the end of 1546: 'There will be a change of religion in England, and the king will take up the gospel of Christ, in case the Emperor should be defeated in this most destructive war [i.e., that against the Schmalkaldic League]: should the gospel sustain a loss, he will then retain his impious mass.' Henry was a statesman first, and a theologian afterwards, like many other men of his century; his religion was very largely a cult of the main chance.

That fact, which not cynicism but sober observation induces the critical historian to see, not only serves to sum up the history of the English Reformation in its Henrician stage, but goes far to explain the unstable state of things which existed when the old king died in January 1547. Though the effects of the religious turmoil raging on the Continent reached England almost from the moment of Luther's revolt, and impinged there upon a situation in which the traditional Catholicism of the country was already shaken by Lollardy and anti-clerical feeling, yet the events which followed were less the result of a national movement than the outcome of a powerful monarchy's natural desire to dominate an hitherto independent Church, and of a series of events which gave it the chance of so doing. As a result, a deep cleavage of theological opinion had been produced, at least in the governing class, and to some extent outside it, and only the strong hand of Henry VIII had prevented either side from carrying its views to their logical end in policy. He had done so on no very clear principle, other than national advantage as Henry saw it. That hand was now to be removed, leaving nothing in its place, for the new King was a minor, and government would have to be carried on by the divided team Henry had unequally yoked together. Could England any longer be isolated from the Continental struggle, independent of Pope and Protestant leaders alike, in the way Henry had tried to keep her? That was the vital question which the new regime would have to answer. And indeed, many of those who were to be vitally concerned in its solution thought the question an unreal one, for they, whose religion was less opportunist than that of their former master, did not consider neutrality in the greatest question of the hour a virtue.

7

Liturgical Change

THEOLOGY can never be a purely theoretical science, and it is therefore vain to imagine that differences in religious outlook can fail to find expression in outward observance. For religion centres in worship, and worship is the expression of belief. It is not surprising to find the divided state of opinion characteristic of the later years of Henry VIII coming to a head in a liturgical controversy in the earlier part of his son's reign. For, from the Protestant point of view, there was much to be objected to in the traditional scheme of worship which, with minor and insignificant changes, had hitherto survived all the upheavals of the period 1529 to 1547. To try to understand these desires for liturgical alterations is perhaps the best approach to the revolution in practical religion which is the central theme of the short but dramatic period between Edward VI's accession in 1547 and his death in 1553.

The central dogma of the Protestant theology was the doctrine of justification by faith only. This stated that the individual soul's relation to God, its translation from the state of being subject to the wrath of its Creator as a member of a fallen race (and a Protestantism, which taught the total depravity of fallen man, regarded this state of alienation far more tragically than did Catholicism), was brought about as a result of a psychological act by which a man accepted Christ consciously as his personal Saviour, not, as Catholic theology taught, by an objective infusion of grace received in the first instance by the sacrament of baptism and developed by the other sacraments. By this act of saving faith the soul was justified, that is, forgiven by God and received into favour with Him, so that nothing short of a complete loss of this attitude of faith could bring about a reversal of the justificatory process. Though other acts of the human personality Godwards, notably charity or the love of God, upon which Catholicism laid stress, were not denied to be desirable, or even necessary, for the advance of man spiritually, yet it was explicitly held by Protestants that these played no part in man's initial salvation. Indeed Luther himself refused to accept the idea that the grace of God fundamentally changed the inner nature of man in the way that medieval theology had taught, and regarded salvation always as due to something added to the natural man, and not the outcome of an ontological transformation of him.

It will be seen that upon such a view the Church and its ministrations played a relatively minor part in religion. For if, as Protestants came to hold, doctrine could be sufficiently derived by each believer from the reading of a self-authenticating Scripture, and if the sacraments did not confer grace, but were rather means of strengthening and confirming saving faith, then there was no need of a Church as the authoritative interpreter of Scripture or as the dispenser of sacramental grace. Moreover any idea that the benefits of the salvation won for man by Christ upon the Cross could be applied to man by his constant joining in a solemn re-presentation of that sacrifice before God in the Mass, as contemporary Catholicism conceived that service to be, was abhorrent to the devotee of the New Learning. For to him the Sacrifice of the Cross was something complete and finished, the benefits of which were appropriated by the individual in his act of saving faith, and he regarded the Mass as a blasphemous attempt to repeat that Sacrifice for particular purposes, an idea in which he was strengthened by some aspects of popular Catholic teaching which did appear to regard each Mass as a new immolation of the Victim of the Cross. (It has been demonstrated that official Catholic theology did not teach this.) If to these considerations (which would need to be extensively developed to make the whole theological crux clear) be added the fact that, whilst Lutheranism had retained a belief in the Real Presence of Christ Himself in the Eucharistic elements, the more radical forms of Protestantism, which were gaining adherents, denied any such association of Christ with the bread and wine, it will be seen how repugnant to holders of the new ideas was the existing form of worship in England. For that centred in the Mass, the liturgy of which and its accompanying ceremonial were designed to express just those beliefs which the Reformers rejected. To a lesser extent this was true of the other services, whether sacramental or not. For the rites of the other sacraments suggested the conferring of grace by sacramental means, which Protestants denied. And the non-sacramental daily cycle of services of praise, known technically as the Divine Office, offended Protestant susceptibilities in other ways; it contained references to practices they considered wrong, such as the invocation of saints, and gave too little prominence to other matters to which they attached great importance, such as the public reading of Scripture. Finally, all services were in the Latin tongue and not the vernacular, and this was intolerable to those who, in conformity with the greater stress they laid upon the psychological processes of personal religion, wished worship consciously to edify the congregation and to be a means of preaching to them.

Consequently the aims of the Protestant liturgical reformers were two-fold. They wished first and foremost to eradicate all in church services which seemed to them to inculcate false ideas. They also wished so to simplify and alter the forms of worship as to make them both more intelligible in themselves and also expressive of the ideas they considered true. This involved a two-fold policy. First and foremost, there must take place the process known at that time as 'turning the Mass into a Communion'. By this was meant the transformation of the Eucharistic service, which, ever since the conversion of England to Christianity, had been the central and principal act of worship, from a ceremony which was regarded chiefly as a sacrifice offered to God by the priest on behalf of and with the cooperation of the people, to one which should, both in words and actions, suggest rather a feast in which the worshippers entered into communion with their Saviour by receiving the eucharistic elements; for this and this alone, was what Protestantism held the Eucharist to be. Secondly, there must be a fairly radical revision and simplification of all the other services, including their translation into everyday language, in such a way that all ideas regarded by Protestants as false would be eliminated and the Gospel, as they conceived it, set forth. This was the aim to which the men of the New Learning had set themselves and, as has been seen, tentative efforts had been made in this direction during the later years of Henry VIII, though they had been almost entirely blocked by the opposition of the Catholic party and the disinclination of the King to allow any but minor changes.

In order to see how circumstances after January 1547 laid the way open to innovation, it is first necessary to examine the political situation at the opening of the new reign. The young King was then just over nine and consequently would not attain his majority for nearly another nine years. His father had provided for the government of the country during this interval by a will, finally executed less than a month before his death. This both determined the succession to the throne in the event of Edward's death without children and appointed a body of eighteen executors of the will, who were described as 'our Privie Councell with our said sonne'. No one executor was given presidential authority, nor was there any provision for the election of a permanent chairman. Decisions were to be made by a bare majority and nothing was said about co-option to fill vacancies. The theory seems to have been the carrying on of government by the legal representatives of a dead king. In opinions about religion this council was divided, though the representatives of the New learning were more numerous than the avowed followers of the Old, and there was also a group who may best be described as *politiques*, more or less neutral in religion and chiefly interested in secular affairs. It must also be noted that some of the extremer conservatives were excluded, the most notable absentee being Bishop Gardiner, their leader upon the episcopal bench. It was said, probably truly, that Henry had deliberately left him out on the ground that, though the old King had felt able to use him because he could control him, he was sure that no one else would be able to do so. Hence the new ruling body was weighted on the side of religious change. It reflects the situation reached, in the ebb and flow of Catholic and Protestant influences in Henry VIII's court, at the moment of his death. The arrest and condemnation of the Duke of Norfolk, the chief lay opponent of Protestantism, had seriously weakened the conservatives, and Gardiner had fallen from favour through suspicion of collusion with Norfolk. It is worth notice that the alleged plot which ruined the Duke was said to include a plan of reconciliation with Rome, so that the religious issue specifically came into the matter. Though the demise of the Crown saved Norfolk from the axe, he remained in prison until Mary's accession and so could play no part in the events of Edward's reign. As things befell, therefore, the change of monarch came at a time peculiarly unfortunate for those who wished to maintain the religious *status quo*, and the revolutionaries gained a start which they were never to lose until 1553.

This was the more important in that the legislation of Henry VIII had given such complete control of the Church, legislative, judicial, and administrative, to the secular government, that whoever had command of that could decide the fate of religion within the limits set by the sixteenth-century equivalent of public opinion, namely the degree to which the country would accept government policy without refusing obedience. As always in the English Reformation, the state held the power, and, now that there was no longer an effective royal sovereign, those who controlled the regency would dictate religious policy.

The immediate arrangements made by Henry VIII lasted a very short while. It is interesting testimony to the force of the principle of personal monarchy in England that it was soon considered inexpedient for the government to hold its authority from the terms of the will. Within three months the original council of regency ceased legally to exist, and was replaced by a new Council, nominally appointed by the boy king and holding its powers theoretically from him. Though it was filled by the same personnel, it was constituted upon a different theory. Already, before this happened, the executors had made Edward Seymour, the new king's uncle, Lord Protector of the Realm. Under the new arrangement, the Duke of Somerset (as he had become) retained this position with almost monarchical powers; he could act without consulting his fellow councillors and could enlarge the Council at his will. Until his fall Protector Somerset was thus legally the regent of England.

This too was significant in the religious sphere, for Somerset was a convinced Protestant. He was a man of mild and conciliatory disposition, who preferred persuasion to force, but there can be no doubt about his sympathies or about his desire to effect changes in matters ecclesiastical. With him at the head of the State supported by a likeminded if more violent group upon the Council, and Archbishop Cranmer in the key position in the Church, there was every likelihood that those changes would be made. From the first the conservative group were reduced to urging that Henry VIII's settlement of religion should be left intact until his son was of age to make his own decisions; they had no hope of preventing, or even of seriously hindering, innovations by their own authority.

For some time little drastic was done. Somerset's cautious and moderate nature, combined with the ambiguous state of foreign affairs, where danger threatened from France, Scotland, and the Empire simultaneously, dictated a slow pace, the arguments for which were strengthened by the divided state of English opinion. Moreover the new king was weak in health and the next heir, Princess Mary, was known to be an uncompromising Catholic. A policy of out-and-out religious revolution was therefore exposed to incalculable risks, even if

Somerset had wished to pursue it without delay. But almost at once signs were obvious of changes to come; sermons were preached against images in churches and there were sporadic instances of iconoclasm. Later in the year the first official steps were taken by the institution of a general visitation of all the dioceses by royal visitors appointed in virtue of the royal supremacy in ecclesiastical affairs. The Injunctions they delivered to the parishes made small but significant alterations in worship, including the introduction of a modicum of English into services. Each church, too, was compelled to accept two books for which the Visitors acted as colporteurs, Erasmus's *Paraphrase of the New Testament*, which ingeniously satirized contemporary religion in retelling the New Testament narrative, and a *Book of Homilies* to be read to the people, which expounded a moderate version of justification by faith only and tacitly ignored such subjects as the Eucharist and other sacraments, whilst attacking in strong terms popular Catholic customs regarded by the Reformers as superstitious. Gardiner attacked the Injunctions and Homilies as contrary to the still legal standards of belief established by Henry VIII and was committed to the Fleet for his pains. The struggle between the partisans of old and new ideas had already begun.

Further steps were taken in the first Parliament of the reign at the end of 1547. (It was probably largely in order to exclude him from this that Gardiner had been imprisoned.) A proposal of Convocation to allow communicants to receive from the chalice was given legislative sanction in an Act which ingeniously strove, by its method of drafting, to reconcile conservative opinion to this change, so much desired by the Reformers, who thought the restriction of the chalice to the celebrating priest unscriptural. The measure contained also penal provisions against those who spoke irreverently of the Sacrament of the Altar. Consequently Catholics shocked by the ribald language already being used by Protestant demagogic preachers, who, with the customary bad taste of sixteenth-century controversialists, were speaking of what was to most Englishmen the Body of Christ as 'Round

Robin' or 'Jack in the box', could hardly vote against the bill without seeming to condone irreverence. Besides this, chantries, the traditional pious foundations which provided money for the regular celebration of Masses for the dead, were confiscated to the Crown. This indeed did no more than complete a policy begun by Henry VIII in 1545 to supply money for the French War, but the preamble to the Act gave as a reason for it that 'a great part of superstition and errors in Christian religion has been brought into the minds and estimations of men, by reason of the ignorance of their very true and perfect salvation through the death of Jesus Christ, and by devising and phantasing vain opinions of purgatory and masses satisfactory, to be done for them which be departed'. It thus cast aspersions upon a prominent feature of popular religion, a feature which, by the practical provisions of the Act, was largely removed. The visible results of this must have struck the public mind with as great a shock as the dissolution of the monasteries, if indeed not a greater one, since chantries were to be found in every large parish church. The money gained by the transaction was, according to the Act, to be devoted to educational and charitable purposes, but, in accordance with a general tendency of this period of the Reformation, most of it went to the nobility who were controlling affairs. A suspicion of this was no doubt what made Cranmer at one stage vote against the bill; for to its religious implications he had no objection.

The year 1548 was largely taken up with what Pollard has called the 'grand national debate' about the Mass and other points of doctrine and practice. There would seem to have been a considered policy on the part of the government to prepare the ground for liturgical changes by influencing public opinion in favour of the Protestant doctrine of the Eucharist. To this end there was an intense propaganda campaign conducted both by press and pulpit. Between twenty and thirty tracts against the Mass are known to have been published during the year, and it is probable that there were others, not now extant. That they were printed with the government's connivance, if not encouragement, is shown by the fact that the printing of books in the contrary sense was hindered, and Gardiner and Tunstall, when they wished to defend the hitherto orthodox doctrine of the Blessed Sacrament, had to publish abroad. The tracts were written in the scurrilous style of contemporary controversy. Thus Anthony Gilby, writes, in answer to Gardiner, that the Papists have 'a carnal change, a carnal presence, a carnal sacrifice; a piece of paste, as we say, flesh and blood as ye say, to be carnally worshipped with fond gestures, a creature to be made a creator, a vile cake to be made God and man'. Just as violent was the language of the team of preachers licensed by the government, who perambulated the country. The pathologically odd Thomas Hancock, whose curious autobiography survives, describes himself as telling a congregation at Salisbury that 'that which the priest holdeth over his head you do see, you kneel before it, you honour it and make an idol of it and you yourselves are most horrible idolaters'. The troubles into which this hot gospeller got himself by his tirades, and the way in which he was rescued, by Somerset's intervention, from prosecution under the Act forbidding reviling of the Sacrament illustrate both the unpopularity of Protestantism in most of the country and the government's complicity in the campaign. Indeed the movement got out of hand; some of the preachers, a proclamation of April 1548 reveals, had been preaching the lawfulness of bigamy. Accordingly the right to issue preaching licence was first restricted to the King, Somerset, and Cranmer, and then disused altogether.

Meanwhile the controversy went on at higher levels still. Distinguished preachers like Latimer preached Protestantism at Paul's Cross, whilst to this year in all probability belongs a questionnaire upon the Mass issued by Cranmer to the bishops, the intention of which can be seen from the fact that some who replied in a Catholic sense were submitted to further interrogatories. Gardiner was summoned to London and ordered to express approval of the official religious policy so far as it had then gone and forbidden to speak of the

Sacrament of the Altar. When he nevertheless affirmed his belief in the Real Presence, he was committed to the Tower, where he remained for the rest of the reign. And at the same time ancient ceremonies, such as the Palm Sunday blessing of palms, had been abolished and all images removed from churches. Both by theory and practice Somerset's administration had been paving the way for a liturgical revolution which would imply a doctrinal one as well.

The first step in this revolution came in 1548 itself, as a result of the legalization of communion in two kinds. For this restoration of ancient practice some liturgical directions were needed, inasmuch as the existing service books did not of course provide for it. So there was issued an *Order of Communion*, giving a series of English prayers of preparation for communion which were to be inserted in the structure of the otherwise unchanged Latin Mass at the point at which the communicants received the elements. This was the first-fruit of the process of liturgical revision which, by the end of the year, was being busily pursued by Cranmer and a committee composed of divines of both schools, though with the New Learning in the majority. By it was brought into being the First Prayer Book of Edward VI, which, by the first Act of Uniformity early in 1549, was made the sole legal form of worship. The passing of the Act was preceded by a full-dress debate upon Eucharistic doctrine in the House of Lords in December 1548, of which the minutes have survived and throw a vivid and curious light upon the outlook of the two parties. As a pretext for the new measure, it was asserted that the differences of liturgical usage which then existed made for confusion, so that henceforth the whole realm was to have but one use. The statement was disingenuous. The relatively small differences between the various local forms of the basically uniform Roman Rite used in medieval England, the Uses of Salisbury, York, Hereford, or Bangor etc., would have hardly been noticeable to any but professional liturgists, and in any case it was the official propaganda that the people had no real understanding of the services at all. As for the other divergences said to be causing bewilderment, they were due to experiments in English services, in such places as the Chapel Royal, which had been connived at by the government. The real object of this plea, which gave the Act of Uniformity its name, apart from the Tudor passion for *Gleichschaltung*, was no doubt a desire not to make too prominent the changes in doctrine which the new book was intended to permit.

For the Prayer Book itself was an ingenious essay in ambiguity. In many ways it was conservative. The general structure of the services, especially of the Mass—the name was retained as a popular and alternative title for what was in strict official parlance henceforth to be called the Communion—was not greatly altered. To the ordinary unlearned worshipper the most obvious change from what was familiar would have been merely the use of the vernacular and the saying aloud of the central Eucharistic prayer or Canon. The old vestments and a number of the old ceremonies were retained. It is when one looks into the actual wording of the prayers that one notices differences. In no case was Catholic doctrine denied by them. But, at every point upon which there was a vital doctrinal difference between the Old Learning and the New, one finds a careful use of words which would enable a Protestant to use the service with a good conscience. Two examples will suffice. In the old Canon of the Mass a prayer just before the consecration of the elements had asked that the bread and wine might 'become unto us' the Body and Blood of Christ; in the new book the phrase is changed to 'that they may be unto us'. The former expression clearly implied some alteration in the nature of the bread and wine; the latter asserted no more than that they were symbols. Or again, the only sacrificial phrase applied to the Eucharist is when it is described as 'this sacrifice of praise and thanksgiving'. This might be understood to mean that the service was a sacrifice *for the purpose of* praise and thanksgiving; but it could equally well mean that it was no more than a metaphorical sacrifice *consisting of* praise and thanksgiving.

That Cranmer himself understood the book in its Protestant sense is clear, both from the line he took in the Lords' debate already mentioned and from his indignant controversy with Bishop Gardiner when the latter, from his cell in the Tower, put a Catholic interpretation upon it. Indeed the final stage in the development of Cranmer's Eucharistic doctrine can be shown, from contemporary evidence, to have taken place in 1548, just before the publication of the book. Hitherto he had believed in a presence of Christ in the elements, originally in the Catholic, later probably in the Lutheran sense—for Lutherans, unlike Zwinglians and Calvinists, had retained a belief in the Real Presence, merely denying that it was brought about by transubstantiation, or the substitution of the inner reality of Christ's Body and Blood for that of the bread and wine. Now Cranmer adopted the more radical notion that the elements were no more than symbols. And, as Cranmer is by common consent the chief author of the new liturgy, it must be supposed that its ambiguities were deliberate, and designed to make room for the tenets the Archbishop shared with other Reformers. Indeed to him the Protestant interpretation was the natural and true one. The fact that a change of doctrine was not made more explicitly must be attributed partly to the pressure of the Henrician Conservatives who served upon the liturgical committee and partly to the fears of the government about the reception the book would have in a country still predominantly of the old way of thinking.

That such fears were not illusory was shown by events. The legal date for the coming into force of the Act of Uniformity was Whit Sunday, 1549. On the very next day a riot, developing into a rebellion, broke out in Devon and spread to Cornwall. It took an army composed largely of German mercenaries and a siege of Exeter to suppress the rising and punish those involved. The alarm caused in London can be seen from the unusually violent sermons preached by Cranmer denouncing the rebels, and from his asperity in the reply he wrote to their formal demands. These were a curious mixture of matters, which illustrate well, both the untheological character of the opposition on the part of country priests and peasants who objected to interference with their old ancient ways, and the firmness with which they rejected the new service which they held to be 'like a Christmas game'. Outside the West Country other risings took place, though here the grievances were by no means exclusively or even perhaps chiefly religious. Indeed Ket's rebellion in Norfolk was wholly concerned with economic matters and its religious ethos was Protestant; the rebels held meetings under an 'Oak of Reformation'. In Oxfordshire there were signs of resentment against the new religion, but there, and elsewhere in the Midlands, the most obvious grievance was enclosure of land. It was the misfortune of Somerset that this perennial sixteenth-century cause of discontent came to a head in the same year that his religious policy first met with serious opposition. He had himself been energetically trying to defeat the enclosing landlords by means of a strict commission of enquiry into their activities, and the hopes and fears thus aroused led to an explosion which coincided in time with the religious discontent. Indeed the two things were probably not unrelated. Some of the opponents of enclosures no doubt associated in their minds Protestantism with the encroachments upon the medieval land system, which now seemed to be more intense, whilst the turmoil of religious controversy which had vexed the whole country in the previous year unsettled men's minds and made them ripe for adventure of any sort.

Whatever the interrelation of their causes, the risings brought about the fall of Somerset. He was accused both of undue leniency in dealing with them and of being responsible for the disorders by his policy of social reform, which had stirred up the commons. Actually the chief cause of his fall was the hatred felt for him by some of his colleagues (notably John Dudley, Earl of Warwick) who were persistent enclosers. His position too had been weakened by the attainder and execution earlier in the year of his brother, Thomas Seymour, who had married Henry VIII's widow, Katharine Parr, and indulged in foolish ambitions of a more or less treasonable nature. In October 1549, therefore, the Duke fell before a coalition headed by Warwick and Wriothesley.

The latter, whom Somerset had earlier removed from the Council, was believed to be a man of Catholic sympathies, although, besides being a notable beneficiary of monastic lands, he seems, after initial resistance, to have accepted Somerset's religious changes, and for a time it was believed that the conspiracy against Somerset would lead to a Catholic reaction. Indeed Warwick, who, before his execution by Mary recanted his Protestantism, might well have taken that line, if he had thought it profitable. Actually, however, having used Wriothesley for his purpose, he dropped him later and dismissed him from the Council, so ending the last hope of a reversal of religious policy. Somerset, who had vainly tried to get the common people to rise on his behalf when he discovered the plot against him, had been sent to the Tower, whence he was released early in 1550, when Warwick felt strong enough to allow him his liberty. But he never regained power, and with his fall ended the attempt to bring in a Protestant establishment of religion by relatively easy stages. For the rest of Edward's reign the pace of religious change quickened, and was too much mixed up with political intrigue and a sordid spoliation of the Church either to win popularity or to be conducted with much regard to purely theological considerations. Somerset had worked with the reforming bishops, and upon principles he shared with them. Warwick, who succeeded him as the mainspring of policy, was a man singularly devoid of sincere principles of any kind and more given to drive both ecclesiastics and laymen than to lead them. His rise to power marks the point at which the religious revolution which had begun gently in 1547 entered upon its Jacobin stage.

8

The Protestant Revolution

MODERN PSYCHOLOGY has shown how frequently fanaticism is the result of doubt; it is the half-believer who needs to reassure himself by a violence which the convinced man eschews. It is perhaps this law of the mind which partly explains the difference between the religious policy of Warwick (now Duke of Northumberland) and that of Protector Somerset, though one may doubt whether the former was ever so much a self-deceived man as a conscious hypocrite. Probably Pollard is right in saying of him that he 'covered his hypocrisy by the vehemence of his protestations'. He was quite certainly sensitive to suspicions of his genuineness, as the remarkable letter to Sir William Cecil shows, in which he expresses his annoyance at the doubts which John Knox, that shrewd Scot, had cast upon his religious zeal.

Master Knox's being here to speak with me, saying that he was so willed by you, I do return him again, because I love not to have to do with men which be neither grateful nor pleasable. I assure you I mind to have no more to do with him but to wish him well, neither also with the Dean of Durham, because, under the colour of a false conscience, he can prettily malign and judge of others against good charity upon a froward judgment. And this matter you might see in his letter, that he cannot tell whether I be a dissembler in religion or not: but I have for twenty years stood to one kind of religion, in the same which I do now profess; and have, I thank the Lord, past no small dangers for it.

The only comment necessary upon this protestation is that

in less than a year from its writing Northumberland was to
die avowing his conversion back to Catholicism, and to speak
of 'false and seditious preachers' as the cause of his heresy.

Whatever the cause, there can be no doubt about the
radicalism of the new head of the administration's proceedings.
He disposed rapidly of the Catholic dupes who had helped
him to power, and the apprehensions, expressed by many of
the reforming party, of a religious reaction were soon shown
to be groundless. Exactly what determined Dudley to throw
in his lot with the left-wing Reformers, rather than with
those who aimed at restoring the position as it was in 1547,
cannot easily be determined. One may suspect it was a
prudent consideration that Protestantism, which eschewed
liturgical splendour and rated the secular power above the
ecclesiastical, offered greater chances of material plunder,
for which the Duke was avid even above his contemporaries.
There was also the fact, whether he perceived it or not, that
violent revolution offers the best opening to dictatorship—a
principle illustrated often enough in history from classical
Greece and Rome down to Napoleonic times and the present
day. And a dictator Northumberland was determined to be.
Already by February 1550 he felt strong enough to release
Somerset from jail, readmit him to the Council, and make him
Earl Marshal. In its outcome the experiment proved that a
despot cannot allow even a fallen predecessor to be above
ground. The ex-Protector opposed the policy of surrender
in foreign affairs which the new government followed, and no
doubt criticized also the wanton pace of religious change at
home. So, on 11 October 1551, he was re-arrested, and
executed next year after a faked trial, in virtue of an extraordinary statute of Northumberland's devising, which made
it treason to assemble twelve persons or more to plot against
the government or to attempt to change the laws relating to
religion, if the assembly kept together for more than an hour
after a proclamation ordering it to disperse had been read.
Even so, the terms of the law seem to have been stretched to
cover Somerset's alleged plot. The truth is that he was a
critic who was dangerous because of his popularity with the

common folk. There was no other leader round whom resistance could gather; the rest of the great nobles either toadied to the new ruler or prudently kept quiet. So, until his last gambler's throw and its failure, Dudley retained his predominance—the more securely in that he seems to have gained the favour of the young King, whom he flattered with a greater measure of freedom from control, and upon whose boyish Protestant bigotry, fostered by education, he played.

The course which religion was destined to take in the hands of this hardy helmsman was soon seen in a series of incidents. The Princess Mary, whose firm refusal to accept the new liturgy had gained for her a tacit liberty to retain the Latin Mass in her own household, was subjected to pressure of persuasion and threats, to such an extent that her Imperial cousin, Charles V, laid plans to rescue her from England by sea. Tudor obstinacy, however, of which she had a full share, and the fear of what Charles might do, enabled her, in spite of petty persecutions of her chaplains and friends, to retain some freedom of worship. A less ambiguous sign was the forced destruction of all the old service books, in order to put material difficulties in the way of any revival of the old liturgy, whilst the mass of church plate, which the new services were held to make redundant, was seized in 1551 to pay the King's debts. It was a rich haul, since the English churches had been famous, as continental visitors bore witness earlier in the century, for the amount and value of their contents. Ecclesiastical revenues began to go the same way, or rather into the pockets of the governing junta. Ponet, who succeeded Gardiner (at length brought to trial and deprived of his see) at Winchester in 1551, had to exchange the rich endowments of the bishopric for an annual stipend of 2,000 marks; a similar bargain was made with Hooper at Gloucester in 1552. The new see of Westminster, one of those founded in the last reign out of dissolved monastic revenues, was suppressed as unnecessary. At the end of Edward VI's reign Northumberland was engaged in a grandiose scheme to substitute for the rich see of Durham two bishoprics of Newcastle and Durham at fixed stipends, leaving the old foundation to become a County Palatine for himself. A more refined form of disendowment was the method of forcing bishops to grant long leases of episcopal manors to courtiers on favourable terms—a policy which impoverished the Church of England until the end of the century, when the leases began to fall in. To the injury of spoliation the dictator added insult. He denounced in Parliament those who spoke against the pillage in their sermons and, in a letter to Cecil, sneered at the reformed clergy:

These men, for the most part, that the King's Majesty hath of late preferred, be so sotted of their wives and children that they forget both their poor neighbours and all other things which to their calling appertaineth; and so will they do so long as his majesty shall suffer them to have so great possessions to maintain their idle lives. Beseeching God that it may be amended.

At the same time he cynically recommended a diplomatic silence before the nation about the degree to which he and others had profited from the Reformation as he understood it. He wrote to Cecil:

We need not to seem to make account to the Commons of his Majesty's liberality and bountifulness in augmenting or advancing of his nobles, or of his benevolence showed to any his good servants, lest you might thereby make them wanton, and give them occasion to take hold of your own arguments; but as it shall become no subject to argue the matter so far, so, if any should be so far out of reason, the matter will always answer itself with honour and reason, to their confuting and shame.

The Circumlocution Office could not have bettered this.

It was against this sordid background of graft and intrigue that measures were set on foot to advance the reform of religion to the degree thought necessary by the extremer Protestants, with whom Northumberland made common cause, and whom he hoodwinked to such an extent they spoke of him with extravagant adulation as a 'valiant soldier of Jesus Christ' and compared him to Scriptural heroes. They had long been dissatisfied with the position established by Somerset, for the ambiguous character of the First Prayer

Book, which was an even greater offence to thorough-going Protestants than to Catholics, was fully grasped at the time. Writing to his friend Bullinger in June 1549, Dryander, one of the Protestant exiles who had come to England, said:

You will see that the summary of doctrine cannot be found fault with, although certain ceremonies are retained in that book which may appear useless, and perhaps hurtful, unless a candid interpretation be put upon them. But in the cause of religion, which is the most important of all in the whole world, I think that every kind of deception either by ambiguity or trickery of language is altogether unwarrantable. You will also find something to blame in the matter of the Lord's Supper; for the book speaks very obscurely, and however you may try to explain it with candour, you cannot avoid great absurdity. The reason is, that the bishops could not of a long time agree among themselves respecting this article, and it was a long and current dispute among them whether transubstantiation should be established or rejected. You perceive therefore by this certain proof, that there are no true and solid principles of doctrine in these men, who take a great deal of pains about the most minute and even absurd matters, and neglect those points on which they ought chiefly to have bestowed their attention.

The ambiguity to which such men took exception was made, to their minds, more serious by the efforts of the conservative clergy to retain all they could of ancient practice, in order to make the changes seem even less than they were and to put a Catholic interpretation upon the new services. St. Paul's Cathedral was a centre of this movement and engaged the attention of the Council: even after the removal of Bonner, who had favoured it, from the see of London, the clergy there and elsewhere in the diocese kept it up. So Nicholas Ridley, Bonner's Protestant successor, enquired in his visitation articles about such matters and gave the following injunctions:

Item, that no minister do counterfeit the popish mass in kissing the Lord's board; washing his hands or fingers after the Gospel or the receipt of the holy communion; shifting the book from one place to another; laying down and licking the chalice after the communion; blessing his eyes with the sudary thereof, or patten,

or crossing his head with the same; holding his forefingers and
thumbs joined together toward the temples of his head, after the
receiving of the sacrament; breathing on the bread or chalice;
saying the Agnus before the communion; shewing the sacrament
openly before the distribution, or making any elevation thereof;
ringing of the sacrying bell, or setting any light upon the Lord's
board. And finally, that the minister, in time of the holy communion, do use only the ceremonies and gestures appointed by
the Book of Common Prayer, and none other, so that there do not
appear in them any counterfeiting of the popish mass.

Another section of the same injunctions illustrates the movement, enthusiastically sponsored by the party of radical
change, to replace the old stone altars, intimately connected
in the mind of the time with an idea of sacrifice, by plain
wooden tables:

Item, Whereas in divers places some use the Lord's board after
the form of a table, and some as an altar, whereby dissention is
perceived to arise among the unlearned; therefore wishing a godly
unity to be observed in all our diocese; and for that the form of a
table may more move and turn the simple from the old superstitious opinions of the popish mass, and to the right use of the
the Lord's supper, we exhort the curates, churchwardens and quest-
men here present to erect and set up the Lord's board after the
form of an honest table decently covered in such place of the quire
or chancel as shall be thought most meet by their discretion and
agreement, so that the ministers with the communicants may have
their place separated from the rest of the people; and to take down
and abolish all other by-tables or altars.

With propaganda, both in word by sermons, and in practice
by such ceremonial changes, going on busily against the
existing liturgy, it was hardly likely that there could fail in
the long run to be further development in official liturgical
rites, especially when it was known that Northumberland
was in favour of this and was using the influence of the
King in the same direction. He could use both English
extremists and foreign divines for his purpose. One of the
features of this period is the extent to which England became a haven of refuge and a field of manœuvre for eminent

Protestant refugees from the Continent. The beginning of Edward VI's reign coincided in time with the victory of Charles V over the Schmalkaldic League at Mühlberg in April 1547, and the consequent introduction of the *Interim*, a measure which ordered the retention of certain Catholic practices in the Empire pending the settlement of religious matters in a General Council. The new policy was considered intolerable by many Reforming divines, who therefore accepted gladly Cranmer's offer of asylum in England. It was one of these, John Laski, a man of Polish origin, who was currently believed to have weaned the Archbishop from the doctrine of the Real Presence, although, on Cranmer's own testimony, Ridley played the major part in this. Many others were now installed in the country, two, Bucer at Cambridge and Peter Martyr at Oxford, in important teaching posts. Their advice was asked in the framing of a new service and had effect in the Second Prayer Book, produced in 1552, though it is noticeable that some of the more conservative suggestions of Bucer for the retention of certain features of the 1549 rite were not accepted—a fact which shows how firmly radical influences were in control, since Bucer represented a tendency to make terms between the more moderate Lutheran type of Protestantism and the extremer Swiss kind, of Zwingli and Calvin, which was having more and more influence upon the English Protestants.

The Second Act of Uniformity, which imposed the new book, like its predecessor, adopted as its ostensible motive a pretext, this time even less ingenuous than the plea of uniformity which had served before. It claimed that ambiguities and doubts about the existing book were one of the causes of its unpopularity, which it admitted in a striking fashion:

Where there has been a very godly order set forth by the authority of Parliament, for common prayer and administration of the sacraments to be used in the mother tongue within the Church of England, agreeable to the Word of God and the primitive church ... And yet this notwithstanding, a great number of people in divers parts of this realm, following their own sensuality, and living either without knowledge or due fear of God, do wistfully and damnably before Almighty God abstain, and refuse to come to their parish churches and other places . . .

Penalties are therefore prescribed for non-attendance and the Act continues:

And because there has arisen in the use and exercise of the afore-said common service in the church, heretofore set forth, divers doubts for the fashion and ministration of the same, rather by the curiosity of the minister and mistakers, than of any worthy cause:

Therefore, as well for the more plain and manifest explanation hereof, as for the more perfection of the said order of common service, in some places where it is necessary to make the same prayers and fashion of service more earnest and fit to stir Christian people to the true honouring of Almighty God, the king's most excellent majesty, with the assent of the Lords and Commons in this present Parliament assembled, and by the authority of the same, has caused the aforesaid order of common service, entitled, The Book of Common Prayer, to be faithfully and godly perused, explained and made fully perfect, and by the aforesaid authority has annexed and joined it, so explained and perfected, to this present statute.

This statement, that the new book merely explained and perfected that of 1549, in fact covered very considerable and drastic changes of the 1549 rite, which made it something very different both in outward appearance and in arrangement and wording. Doctrinally, the assertion does probably des-cribe fairly accurately what was aimed at. As we have seen, the vital change in Cranmer's Eucharistic beliefs had come before 1549, and the First Prayer Book was intended to be at least compatible with his new ideas. When Gardiner, in a paper dispute about the doctrine of the Eucharist conducted from prison with his Metropolitan, had claimed that the Book expressed Catholic doctrine, Cranmer had indignantly main-tained that Gardiner's interpretation was wrong. Now he was able to make his intention clear by so rearranging the service as to eliminate some of the features to which appeal had been made. The structure of the new Communion rite was very different from the older order, which had reproduced the plan of the Latin Mass. The former central Eucharistic prayer was now split into three separated portions to remove any suggestion of a solemn sacrificial approach to God and the prayers relating to the communion of the people were placed before the consecration of the bread and wine, as if to indicate that communion alone was the purpose of consecration. The language was changed in detail, and always in such a way as to make Protestant ideas more prominent. More significant still to the ordinary worshipper, the ceremonial was made much plainer; the old vestments, historically associated with the old ideas, were no longer to be used and the communion table, which replaced the altar, was to be placed with its ends east and west in the chancel or body of the church, the officiant standing on the north side of it instead of altar-wise. These, and the changes in the other services, approximated the English service, both in language and ceremonial, much more closely to Continental Protestant rites of the Swiss type and effectually prevented the methods by which conservative priests had been making the new order resemble the old Mass, in the ways objected to by Ridley. The Second Prayer Book was thus a powerful instrument in promoting the liturgical aims of the Reformers, though it still did not go far enough for the extremists. Thus, at the last moment, some of them tried to have the practice of kneeling to receive communion, which they took to imply adoration of the Sacrament, abolished. Though exasperated by this demand, Cranmer consented to the insertion, after the Book was in the press, of a note (the famous 'Black Rubric'), explicitly denying that any such adoration was intended or justifiable.

It seemed, therefore, as if Protestantism in its most radical form had triumphed in England, and as if the revolution, which had gone on with increasing momentum since 1547, was about to be consummated. But now time was working against the Reformers. The Protestant revolution had been made possible only by the accession of a minor to the throne, and its continuance was bound up with the life of Edward VI, which, it was becoming obvious, would not be prolonged. As the King's health weakened, the problem of the succession became acute. Mary was, by Henry VIII's disposition, the next heir. She had never dissembled her Catholicism, and it was clear that her coming to the throne would be the signal for a return to the religious situation of 1547, if not further back still. That was enough to alarm any Protestant, especially in an age when tolerance was unknown, and indeed thought wrong. To Northumberland the prospect was still more critical. His tyranny depended upon his dominance of the Council, and upon the ascendancy he seems to have acquired over the boy king. An adult sovereign, especially one with the Tudor taste for personal rule, would in any case end his supremacy. But Mary had especial cause to hate him, as the agent of the most drastic stage of the religious *bouleversement*, as one who had harried her personally in her religious practices, and as an upstart of recent nobility— which was a real offence to her half-Spanish sense of birth and blood. Hence the Duke's position, and probably his life, depended upon an effort to divert the succession.

To do this was not an easy task. Northumberland was an unpopular man in the country, feared by his colleagues, hated by all who had revered Somerset, and the ogre of all Catholics. There was little or no chance of his being accepted as King himself, though the French Ambassador, who feared Mary as being closely related to Charles V, suggested usurpation. Elizabeth, heir next after Mary, would hardly serve his turn; she had enough of her father in her to make it unlikely that she would let Northumberland be the power behind the throne. Mary of Scotland, who was a great-grand-daughter of Henry VII, would be unacceptable for her French connexions, and as a Catholic. So Northumberland, if he was to take into account the strong feeling of Englishmen for an hereditary monarchy, was almost compelled to turn to the Grey family, who were descended from Henry VIII's younger sister, the elder Mary Tudor. It was from these considerations that the plot, which was to end in the short reign of Lady Jane Grey, took its rise.

In the time which remained before the death of Edward

in the summer of 1553 the Reforming party carried on their campaign with very little attention to the developing crisis. Cranmer's chief interest was his plan for building up a united international Protestantism to oppose the neo-Catholicism which seemed likely to emerge from the Council of Trent. This body had begun its sessions and was seen to be giving a new precision to Catholic doctrine upon all the points in dispute with the Reformation, without serious thought of compromise. As against this growing united front, Protestantism, rent by the quarrels between Lutherans and the Swiss Reformers, was weak and divided, whilst its opponents, already more vigorous as the result of the work of new religious orders like the Jesuits, could count upon the support of the Emperor and perhaps on that of other Catholic princes. England, already the haven of refuge, could, Cranmer hoped, be the centre of unity for the Reformation. So one finds him in correspondence with Calvin and others urging agreement.

It was a difficult task. Protestantism, from its very appeal to private judgement, was bound to be fissiparous. How far the left wing were already going in the rejection even of central doctrines of historic Christianity can be illustrated from a letter of Hooper's, written in June 1549 after his return to England:

The anabaptists flock to the place and give me much trouble with their opinions respecting the incarnation of the Lord; for they deny altogether that Christ was born of the virgin Mary according to the flesh. They contend that a man who is reconciled to God is without sin, and free from all stain of concupiscence, and say nothing of the old Adam remains in his nature; and a man, they say, who is thus regenerate cannot sin. They add that all hope of pardon is taken away from those who, after having received the Holy Ghost, fall into sin. They maintain a fatal necessity, and that beyond and besides that will of his which he has revealed to us in the scriptures, God hath another will by which he altogether acts under some kind of necessity. Although I am unable to satisfy their obstinacy, yet the Lord by his word shuts their mouths, and their heresies are more and more detested by the people. How dangerously our England is afflicted by heresies of this kind, God only knows; I am unable indeed from sorrow of heart to express to your piety. There are some who deny that man is endued with a soul different from that of a beast, and subject to decay. Alas! not only are those heresies reviving among us which were formerly dead and buried, but new ones are springing up every day. There are such libertines and wretches, who are daring enough in their conventicles not only to deny that Christ is the Messiah and Saviour of the world, but also to call that blessed Seed a mischievous fellow and deceiver of the world.

Hooper was always a fanatic, who took a jaundiced view of things, but there is sufficient evidence to show that his picture was not hopelessly exaggerated. The Reforming party had had in a few cases to deal with some of the aberrations springing from extreme Protestant individualism by persecution. And the controversies among relatively orthodox Protestants went deep enough, especially the Eucharistic dispute. Hooper once again is an example of the bitterness of feeling; whilst still in exile in 1546 he had written to Bullinger:

The count Palatine has lately provided for the preaching of the gospel throughout his dominions: but as far as relates to the eucharist he has descended, as the proverb has it, from the horse to the ass; for he has fallen from popery into the doctrine of Luther, who is in that particular more erroneous than all the Papists; and those who deny the substance of bread to remain in the sacrament, and substitute the body of Christ in its place, come more closely to the truth than those who affirm that the natural body of Christ is with the bread, in the bread, and under the form of bread, and yet occupies no space. God I hope will at length give him a better mind.

In such circumstances a united Reformation was a vain hope. Nor was Cranmer the best person to attempt to secure it. Though pacificatory by temperament, and singularly moderate in his exposition of the central Protestant tenet of justification by faith only, he had all the zeal of a convert in the Eucharistic controversy. It would seem that there is little to be said for the old view that he was an adherent of the mediating view of Bucer, who, although he denied a presence in the elements, vainly tried to reconcile Lutherans and Zwinglians by using the phrase 'real presence' of Christ's body received by faith by the communicant. Cranmer declined to accept Bucer's views in some vital points of liturgical revision and, in his last doctrinal formulary, the Forty-Two Articles of 1553, which he drew up for acceptance by all licensed preachers, he denied categorically even the abstract possibility of any Real Presence of Christ on earth before the Last Judgement.

Forasmoche as the trueth of mannes nature requireth, that the bodie of one and the selfsame manne cannot be at one time ine diverse places, but must nedes be in some one certeine place: Therfore the bodie of Christe cannot bee presente at one time in many and diverse places. And because (as holie Scripture doeth teache) Christe was taken up into heaven, and there shall continue unto thende of the worlde, a faithful man ought not, either to beleve or openlie to confesse the realle and bodilie presence (as thei terme it) of Christes fleshe and bloude in the Sacramente of the Loordes supper.

Such a statement could lead only to a permanent breach between right- and left-wing Protestantism, and was no hopeful sign for the cause which the Archbishop had at heart. Actually however its effect was never to be tried, for the Articles were issued as the political crisis began which both ended in the succession of a Catholic sovereign and involved the Reforming party in the odium of an attempt to defeat the lawful devolution of the English crown.

By the time Edward VI finally died Northumberland had his plans complete. He had fixed upon Lady Jane Grey as his destined puppet Queen and had married her to his son, Guilford Dudley, so that, like Banquo, the Duke might have begotten kings though not able to be one himself. By working upon the sincere and fanatical Protestantism in which Edward VI had been brought up, he persuaded the boy to make a will setting aside his father's plans and nominating the Lady Jane and her descendants as his heirs; only so, the King was persuaded, could Popery be prevented from returning to England and the Gospel secured. By threats and intimidation Northumberland then forced those men of prominence who had not already thrown in their lot with him to affix their signatures to the document, including Cranmer, who, with his strong belief in legitimacy and divine right, was peculiarly loath to do so and resisted for some time. Then, when Edward died, Ridley was persuaded to preach at Paul's Cross that Mary was a bastard, and Jane was proclaimed Queen.

It was the last throw of a daring gambler and it failed speedily. Northumberland had not been able to secure Mary's person in time; warned of what was happening she took refuge on the Duke of Norfolk's estates and there was joined by an increasing number of nobles and their followers. It was not by any means zeal for the old religion which rallied England to her support, as is shown by the fact that her base of operations was the Eastern counties, where Protestantism was strongest, though discontent with religious changes played its part. Hatred of Northumberland and his junta, and the deep-seated English sentiment for hereditary monarchy, strengthened as that was by the dynastic quarrels of the last century and the Tudor gift of orderly government, were the dominant motives. Gardiner, in the sermon which cost him his liberty, had given expression to a popular feeling when he said that he misliked subjects 'that would take upon them to rule like kings, to the diminishing of the King's dignity and the confusion of their own estate'. Men were tired of oligarchic rule. Northumberland noted the lack of enthusiasm for his cause when he rode out of London to face Mary's forces, and, in the field, he found his troops unable to do anything in the face of her growing power. Behind his back the Council realized the hopelessness of maintaining a cause into which they had been dragooned by their imperious leader and themselves proclaimed Mary. The Duke himself tried to go with the tide by proclaiming her in Cambridge market-place, but was speedily arrested and brought back to London, which Mary entered in triumph to the plaudits of a city which was quite soon to show among many of its citizens a reluctance to return to her religion.

Northumberland's adventure in power was over and with it ended too the whole experiment of a Protestant revolution accomplished by a minority which, owing to the accidents of politics, possessed supreme power. Far too much had been attempted in a brief period of six years, and the inevitable reaction was to follow. But, as so often, the event proved that a revolutionary interlude could not be ignored or a return made to the exact *status quo ante*. It was not only the mistakes of Mary's regime which defeated her attempts to re-establish the state of things which she regarded as right. The events of 1547 to 1553 had unleashed forces which could never again be wholly brought under control. Though a time of minority rule, that period had both given the Protestant cause the unforgettable experience of power and success and had exacerbated feeling between the two religions in England to a degree which made future compromise or settlement a matter of difficulty, if not of impossibility. There had seemed some hope of stability in the Henrician settlement, makeshift as that was. Stability could not easily be looked for after the reign of Edward VI.

9

The Marian Reaction

IT WAS THE TRAGEDY of Mary Tudor to be a logical woman in an illogical and confused situation. Inheriting through her mother the stern, reasoned, Catholic orthodoxy characteristic of Spain, an orthodoxy at this very time bearing its greatest fruits in the great sixteenth-century Spanish theologians, she probably never understood, still less sympathized with, the confused and instinctive English approach to the Reformation and Counter-Reformation. Hers was the spirit which had inspired the long Spanish crusades against the Moors—a simple-minded attitude, which saw everything in terms of black and white; 'Christians are right and pagans are wrong,' as the Song of Roland put it, in dealing with an episode of that struggle. It was a very different outlook from that of English Catholicism, which, until Lollardy appeared in the late fourteenth century, had never been conscious of any challenge to its beliefs and could afford to be easy-going. Add to this the tradition of absolution derived from a father she had always revered, despite his treatment of her, and the influence of a frustrated youth, separated at an early age from her mother and condemned for years to ignominy, and one begins to understand the factors which moulded Mary, and which account for most of the mistakes of her reign. She was one whose inherited qualities and early experiences alike unfitted her for the role which unkind fate condemned her to play, in a situation which would have taxed the best equipped stateswoman of the time.

The palmary mistake she made was, probably, to mis-interpret the wave of genuine and spontaneous enthusiasm which carried her to the throne and greeted her assumption of it. To her, who saw everything in the light of the rather severe type of Catholic faith which was her deepest senti-ment, it was the reaction of a people robbed of its religion and welcoming in her the restoration of Catholicity. In reality, as we have seen, this was a shortsighted view of the situation; a great part of the loyalty which confounded Northumberland's plot was rather an expression of patriotic devotion to the hereditary principle and to the dynasty enshrining it—a dynasty which had not hitherto been con-spicuous for Catholic orthodoxy. It was not so much Mary's religion, as her ancestry, and the fact that she symbolized the end of gangster government, which commended her to the nation as a whole. But from this initial misreading of the facts sprang a whole chain of errors.

Not that Mary erred at first by undue severity. Few mon-archs of her time, after the defeat of a conspiracy to deprive them of their birthright, would have acted so magnanimously. Apart from Northumberland and his most immediate cronies no one was put to death. The exculpations of themselves put forward by the *politiques* who had acquiesced in his plot were accepted—that of Cecil was a masterpiece of ingenious glossing of facts—and some of them were retained upon the unwieldy Council of too many members, which was to be Mary's instrument of government and a source of weakness, owing to its factious and intriguing personnel, throughout her reign. Even Cranmer, whom Mary must have regarded both as a pastor unfaithful to his charge and as the means of her mother's putting away, as well as a traitor, was left at liberty until, in answer to a ridiculous rumour that he had offered to say Mass before the Queen, he unwisely allowed a violent placard against the Mass (probably not of his own composition) to be put out in his name. And, in matters of religion, she began by a tolerant and persuasive policy which went beyond that of Somerset. The Queen, said a proclama-tion of August 1553, 'cannot now hide that religion, which

God and the world know she has ever professed from her infancy hitherto; which as her majesty is minded to observe and maintain for herself by God's grace during her time, so doth her highness much desire, and would be glad, the same were of all her subjects quietly and charitably embraced'. It went on to say that she would use no compulsion in the matter 'unto such time as further order, by common assent may be taken therein'. Therefore Mary wishes her 'good loving subjects' to 'live together in quiet sort and Christian charity, leaving those new-found devilish terms of papist or heretic and such like'. The only orders given are that irregular preaching and unlicensed printing must stop and that no private reprisals must be taken against the Duke of Northumberland's party, though information against the traitors will be accepted, if proffered.

The 'further order' referred to here was taken in Mary's first Parliament, which passed a comprehensive Act of Repeal, annulling all the religious legislation of her brother's reign and, as far as possible, restoring the religious position of 1547:

Forasmuch as by divers and several Acts hereafter mentioned, as well the divine service and good administration of the sacraments, as divers other matters of religion, which we and our forefathers found in this Church of England, to us left by the authority of the Catholic Church, be partly altered and in some part taken from us, and in place thereof new things imagined and set forth by the said Acts, such as a few of singularity have of themselves devised, whereof has ensued amongst us, in very short time, numbers of diverse and strange opinions and diversities of sects, and thereby grown great unquietness and much discord

—therefore the Edwardine statutes enumerated are repealed and it is ordered that church services shall be as they were in the last year of Henry VIII. This was the perfect expression of the attitude of the Henrician religious conservatives, by whose influence it was no doubt carried, though not without opposition. They disliked, and wished to do away with, novelties which had supplanted the religion of their childhood, to which they attributed the theological wrangling and political disturbances from which Mary's advent had, it seemed, delivered them. But they were by no means so ready to undo the work of her father. Cardinal Pole, whom the Pope had appointed Legate for the purpose of the re-conciliation with England which he hoped and expected to take place, wished the Queen at once to abandon the royal supremacy in matters of religion, a supremacy which she herself disliked in conscience retaining, but Gardiner and the Council opposed such a precipitate move. There was in fact no enthusiasm for papal authority as such among most Englishmen, and the Royal Supremacy, provided that it was exercised to maintain what they wanted, did not grate unduly upon the feelings even of the Catholically minded. Here was one example of the clash between Mary's Spanish logicality and English empiricism which was to become even more apparent later. In practice, compromise was reached by the tacit disuse of the royal title of 'Supreme Head', masked by a convenient 'etc.' in the royal style, and the use of the supre-macy to restore the old ways. This was in fact the funda-mental paradox of the reign: a restoration which was eventually to bring back the Pope was carried out by means of an authority originally set up to supplant the Papacy. In the next reign Jewel was to retort to Harding, who taunted the Elizabethan Church with a 'parliament religion', that in Mary's day the Papists had had a 'parliament Pope', and him under conditions, 'otherwise his holiness had gone home again'. It was a true statement of the case, for the Marian settlement, no less than the Henrician, the Edwardine, and the Elizabethan, rested upon statute law, not upon the tacit recognition of a supposed nature of things. Mary's mind about the independence of the Church was sufficiently shown in the Royal Injunctions of 1554, which ordered the bishops to restore the authority of the canons not expressly contrary to the laws of the realm, not to use in their formal documents the phrase *Regia auctoritate fulcitus*, and not to demand from anyone the legal oaths against papal authority. But the very fact that these instructions to resume inherent episcopal authority came in the form of royal orders similar in form to those of Henry VIII and Edward VI, if different in style and content, betrayed a fact which no disuse of titles could conceal, namely that the broken autonomy of the Church could now only be patched together by State influence; only the power which had deposed the self-governing Church could restore it, and then only for so long as State policy remained constant.

The same Injunctions prescribed an interim policy for religious reaction. 'Sacramentaries' (i.e., disbelievers in the Real Presence) and other heretics were not to be admitted to benefices, and married priests (the Edwardine legalization of clerical marriage having been repealed) were to be removed from their cures, though clerical widowers and those willing to put away their wives and to do penance were to be pardoned. Finally, taking a leaf from the Protestant book, it was recommended that bishops should put out collections of homilies, to be read to the people in church with a view to bringing them back to orthodox belief. For the moment, however, no more violent steps than these to crush Protestantism were undertaken.

A mild and gradual policy of this kind might well have eventually succeeded in the objects Mary had at heart, had it not gone hand in hand with a capital mistake of the reign, the Spanish marriage. It was the fate of Mary, as it was to be that of James II later, to link her religion in people's minds with an unpopular alliance with foreigners. Mary was no self-confident feminist and she distrusted her own power to rule England, as its first woman sovereign, alone; she desired a husband to wear the crown matrimonial and take some of the burden of government off her shoulders. So far as that desire went, most of her people would probably have supported her; to them too an unmarried Queen seemed an anomaly, and, though some welcomed the idea of Elizabeth as her successor, to many an undisputed male heir in the direct line would have been welcome. An English husband for the sovereign, provided he seemed a worthy one, would have been accepted. But Mary looked further afield. She may have inherited the Spanish sense of rank, which would disapprove of the idea of marrying a subject; in any case she listened with favour to the proposal of marriage with Philip of Spain, heir to Charles V, put forward with all the skill of the Emperor's ambassador, Simon Renard. Not only did Philip belong to her mother's family; he was part and parcel of the great power which Charles V had built up in Europe by his union of the Habsburg and Spanish inheritances, even though not destined to succeed to all of it. That power, too, was the most rigidly Catholic of any in Europe—far more so than France, where Huguenotism was already developing, which under Francis I had on more than one occasion been willing to lend countenance to Henry VIII's attempts to bring pressure upon the Pope. And so it was the Spanish match which eventually carried the day against all alternative suggestions.

To understand the popular dislike of it it is necessary to remember the international situation of the day. Europe was divided between the rival ambitions of France and the Spanish-Imperial combination. England was weak; her finances were in an almost desperate situation, despite the confiscations of church property, and militarily she was negligible. There was therefore no hope or question of being able to maintain a dominant position on the Continent; the chief requirement indeed was to keep out of foreign adventure in order to eliminate danger of invasion. The one way in which England could exercise influence was to be an unattached entity for whose graces the big powers might be prepared to make advances and bid against each other. To attach the country to one or other of the big agglomerations of power, always in a potentially hostile relationship to each other, was to invite reprisals from the other, and perhaps also domination from the chosen ally. It was this last aspect of an alliance with Spain which bulked largest in the popular mind. Mary's husband would be King of England, and, whatever precautions might be taken in advance, that would mean Spanish domination of the country. So ran the popular argument, assisted by propaganda from the influential men who were opposed to the union. In the investigations into the origin of Wyatt's rebellion one specimen of the rumours which induced men to rise came to light, in the form of a statement that 'the Spaniards were coming into the realm with harness and hand-guns, and would make us Englishmen worse than enemies, and viler'; and this was probably typical of many such utterances. What was known of the Spanish Inquisition, an institution under State control and therefore more efficient and ruthless than the ordinary papal Inquisition, probably added to the fears of the many who did not see eye to eye with the Queen in matters of religion. And to all was added the English hatred of foreigners, an unreasoning xenophobia often remarked by foreign visitors, something which went back at least to the thirteenth century and had been fanned almost to madness by the isolation from Europe caused by Henry VIII's schism.

It was not Protestants alone who objected. Mary's Catholic advisers, including Gardiner, were opposed; Parliament raised its voice and it was commonly thought at the French Court that Charles V was preventing Cardinal Pole from proceeding to England 'fearing lest he should go about to let this marriage of the Queen and the Prince of Spain'. The agitation was assisted by the French Ambassador, who had a professional interest in keeping Mary from alliance with Spain, and early in 1554 it led to the outbreak of Wyatt's rebellion in Kent, a rising which reached London before collapsing. Wyatt had Protestant sympathies and his strength was drawn from the south-eastern part of the country in which the new religion was strongest, but it is interesting to notice a story that when a Kentish gentleman who joined him said, 'I trust you will restore the right religion again,' the rebel leader replied, 'Whist! Ye may not so much as name religion, for that will withdraw from us the hearts of many: you must only make your quarrel for overrunning of strangers. And yet to thee be it said in counsel, as unto my friend, we mind only the restitution of God's word.' As yet there was no sign of general revolt against the Marian religious policy, despite disturbances in London which had accompanied the first changes.

The suppression of the revolt hardened the government and led to the execution of the unfortunate Jane Grey and her husband, who had hitherto merely been kept in the Tower, but it did not modify the Queen's policy. Mary had her full share of Tudor persistency against opposition and the marriage finally took place in Winchester Cathedral on 25 July 1554, soon after Philip's landing at Southampton. He had been fully warned of the feeling against him and his countrymen which still persisted. In March Renard had written to Charles V:

Sire—Wher I consider the state of things here, the condition of the Queen and this kingdom, the confusions in religion, the different parties amongst the Privy Councillors, the intestine hatred between the nobility and the people, the character of the English—who are given so much to change, treason, and infidelity—the natural enmity they bear to strangers, and all that from one time to another they have done against them,—which, too, is increased, especially against Spaniards, by the French intrigues and the evil reports spread by your Majesty's own subjects; and when, on the other side, I call to mind of what consequence it is that His Highness should not be thrown in any peril, on whose safety so many kingdoms, and countries, and so many people depend and are supported; and moreover, when I look to the difficulty there is to get any pledges from the English on which we may rely;—having all this before me, I feel the burden of this charge so heavy, its importance so great, that I know not in what way to satisfy or be conformable to the commands your majesty has sent me by your last letters.

So Philip, by a show of tact and respect for English traditions, did what he could to ingratiate himself with his new subjects. But it was ominous that brawls between the people and his Spanish servants soon broke out, caused by the insolence which the English felt they detected in the intruding foreigners.

The settlement of the marriage question appeared to leave the way clear for the further measures in religion which Mary, supported now by Philip, wished to take, namely the complete ending of the schism between England and Rome and the restoring of the old relations of Church and State as they had been in 1529. This was a far more difficult proposal to which to gain assent from the representatives of the nation than had been the overthrowing of Edwardine innovations. It was a theoretical matter only to many who had felt strongly the loss of their old services and rejoiced to have them back. There was still a sentimental affection for the memory of Henry VIII, whose work was now to be undone, an affection perhaps all the stronger now that his heavy hand was a memory only. For over twenty years now the Pope had been officially no more than 'the Bishop of Rome' in England and a zealous and continued propaganda had denounced his claims as bogus, whilst the anti-clerical feeling which had long preceded the Reformation remained, ready to be stirred to life by any suggestion of the revival of the medieval system of ecclesiastical independence and control over the laity under the aegis of a foreign prelate. Finally, there was an economic motive of the most obvious kind which operated most strongly with the temporal peers of Parliament and with many of those who made up the Lower House—the matter of the abbey lands. Would reconciliation with Rome involve their return to the Church? This was not wholly the anxiety of looters; many or most of the then holders of the confiscated property had paid the Crown for their share, and in some cases it had passed to purchasers who played no part in the Dissolution.

It was not until this last question had been settled, by a promise that the Pope would condone the alienation of former church property, that the far-reaching second Act of Repeal of 1554 (1 & 2 Philip and Mary, cap. 8) was passed, by which, as far as could be done, the whole train of events from 1529 onwards was reversed. The statute recites the story of the schism, and the fact of Pole's legateship; it enrols a solemn expression of sorrow made by Parliament for all that had happened and records the Cardinal's formal act of absolution of the realm from the censures incurred and restoration of it to Catholic unity. This, it states, had been done on the faith of a promise of the repeal of all anti-papal statutes, which the Act then proceeds to repeal in detail. It then goes on to record a request by Parliament that Pole would by 'dispensation, toleration or permission respectively, as the case shall require' make a series of concessions. He was asked to confirm ecclesiastical foundations (such as the new bishoprics) made since the schism, marriages contracted without the papal dispensations ordinarily required for validity, ecclesiastical preferments granted, and judgements of ecclesiastical courts made during the times of schism and, finally, to secure to the present possessors all alienated church lands. Convocation had already been asked to renounce whatever claims the English clergy had to them and their act of condonation is included in the Act. That document contains an interesting statement of the reasons which moved the clergy to this act of grace:

We freely confess ourselves to know well how difficult and almost impossible would be the recovery of ecclesiastical possessions on account of the many and almost inextricable contracts and dis-posals made thereof, and that should it be attempted, the peace and tranquillity of the realm would be easily disturbed, and the unity of the Catholic Church—which now, by the piety and authority of your majesties, is in this kingdom introduced—would, with the greatest difficulty, be able to obtain its due progress and end.

In return, the clergy ask for the restoration of their ecclesiastical authority.

The Act then recites Pole's dispensation authorizing all these concessions; as a *quid pro quo* the Legate asks only that those who hold church moveables shall restore them to the pillaged churches and that out of the ecclesiastical possessions they retain they shall provide proper stipends for the clergy. The whole arrangement is then confirmed by the authority of Parliament and the title of the Crown to its own share of ecclesiastical property is given legal security. Then the legislators go on to some interesting provisions which show clearly their state of mind. As the royal title of Supreme Head is necessarily abandoned by the repeal of the Henrician Acts, it is enacted that royal documents containing it shall still have force, even though the title has always, according to the view of papal authority now accepted again, been invalid. Mary's extra-legal dropping of it is also given retro-spective Parliamentary authority—'And where your highness, sovereign lady, since your coming to the crown of this realm, of a good and Christian conscience, omitted to write the said style of supremacy', documents so worded are validated. Papal bulls are given once again legal force—but only those 'not containing matters contrary or prejudicial to the autho-rity, dignity or pre-eminence royal or imperial of the realm, or to the laws of this realm now being in force, and not in this present Parliament repealed'. As an act of grace the provisions of the Mortmain Statutes, by which alienation of land to ecclesiastical corporations was limited, are suspended for twenty years to allow of the re-endowment of churches. A final provision declares that nothing in the Act diminishes the royal prerogative and that papal authority is restored in England as it was in the earlier days of Henry VIII 'without diminution or enlargement of the same'.

It is worth thus considering the Act in detail, in order to see the way in which unconditional surrender to the Papacy was avoided, even in the very process of making submission, and how inevitably even this attempted return to the medieval polity rested upon the sovereignty of Parlia-ment. In strict medieval theory most of the matters legislated about were outside the authority of Parliament or of the secular power. But the very form of the Henrician proceedings made it unavoidable that anti-papal legislation should be undone by the power which passed it. It is in such ways that revolutions impose their form even upon counter-revolutions; Jewel's description of the Marian settlement as involving a 'parliament Pope' was justified by the mere fact that no other machinery could be devised under the English constitution to reseat Peter upon his throne.

But, whatever their legal form, counter-revolutions usually call for victims and this one was no exception. The perse-cution, which was to be the best-remembered feature of Mary's reign in later times, was late in starting, but once begun went on to its end. At first the government, so far from wanting blood, had encouraged both immigrant foreign

Protestants and native dissidents to flee the country. Gardiner related with pride his method of inducing them to remove themselves by a summons to his presence which left ample time to escape. It was, too, in the earlier part of the reign, before the fires of Smithfield were started, that there took place that exodus of some of the more prominent Protestants which recent research has shown to have been something of an organized emigration, designed to prepare for more favourable times, rather than a panic flight. It was directed by Cecil and others destined to be key men under Elizabeth, and served its purpose, in that it provided a nucleus of trained persons to inaugurate the reaction after 1558. The predominant motive is well expressed in a letter of Cranmer's in which he speaks of fleeing 'the infection of the antechristian [*sic*] doctryne by departure oute of the realme'. The Reforming party wished some at least of their number to avoid absorption into the new order by exile. The *émigrés* settled in colonies in different towns of Germany and Switzerland, some also going to France. It was at Frankfurt that there took place, in one of the most interesting of these self-exiled groups, the disputes between those who wished to stick to the letter of the Second Edwardine Prayer Book in worship and those who desired more radical liturgical changes, which were the genesis of the Elizabethan quarrels between Puritans and Anglicans. Already the divisions of the next period of the English Reformation were beginning.

There were, however, many who remained, some to be caught eventually in the toils of the heresy trials which the revival of the old anti-Lollard statutes in November 1554, and the revival of independent ecclesiastical jurisdiction, made almost inevitable. Who urged on the policy of burning has often been disputed. The popular idea that it was Philip must be abandoned in view of the evidence that his father urged leniency, and that one of his Spanish ecclesiastical entourage actually preached at court in February 1555 (the very month in which the execution of John Rogers began the policy of the stake) against burning for heresy. Equally the Protestant myth of the blood-thirstiness of Gardiner and

Bonner among the bishops does not square with the evidence. To the Queen herself must probably be attributed the motive force behind the policy, though it must be remembered that all concerned, Philip, Mary, the bishops, and the Council, shared, in theory at least, the sixteenth-century view that religion must be maintained by the coercing of heretics, by death if need be, and that none of them were likely to oppose it on principle. It was in fact in the nature of things that the restoration of pre-Reformation ecclesiastical authority should be accompanied by the carrying out of canonical provisions for persecution, which indeed had been continued under other legal forms under Henry VIII and Edward VI.

What was distinctive about the Marian persecution was the application once again of the old tests of heresy, which amounted to its definition as any dissent from the standards of the Roman Church, and the quality of the victims, many of whom were humble folk, artisans and others. It was this probably which most of all moved public opinion to sympathy, and ensured the passing of the fires into a national tradition, which, embalmed in Foxe's hagiography, *The Book of Martyrs*, was to keep alive hatred of Popery for generations. The Tudor populace was used to spectacular executions of great men, whether for religion or politics, and regarded them both as public entertainments and as part of the hazards of greatness which ordinary folk escaped. 'Mercy will soon pardon the meanest: but mighty men shall be mightily tormented.' It was a different thing when commoners like themselves were put to death in numbers with every circumstance of judicial horror, especially when the capital was the scene of many such martyrdoms. In any case there is no doubt of the increasing revulsion of feeling which accompanied the progress of the burnings. They gave to the Protestant party a sympathy which had been wholly lacking to them in the days of their power under Edward VI, and they were one of the factors which prevented the Elizabethan settlement from being as much of a compromise between the two faiths as it might otherwise have been.

It was not only, however, the little men who perished.

Besides notable Protestant preachers, four Edwardine bishops, Latimer, Ridley, Hooper, and Ferrar, were burnt, and the culminating victim was Archbishop Cranmer, who went to the stake at Oxford in the spring of 1556. Although convicted of high treason in November 1553, for his share in Northumberland's attempt to make Lady Jane Grey Edward VI's successor, he had been kept from an earlier death, partly because his position as Archbishop was held to require authority from Rome to try and sentence him, and partly through his surrender to human weakness which induced him to recant the doctrines for which he was condemned until his final avowal of faith on his way to the stake. His constancy at the end, after previous recantation, was a heavy blow to the government's prestige, which would have been heightened had he died professing repentance. His case, too, is of great and pathetic interest to the student of contemporary opinion for the extraordinary dilemma in which his high belief in royal ecclesiastical supremacy placed him, when he was commanded by the laws of a Papist king and queen to acknowledge the jurisdiction of the Pope. He had ever held that the Crown had by divine right the power to determine questions of religion. What was he to do when the Crown ordered him to accept something his conscience told him was untrue? Grotesque as the problem must seem to all who do not share his notion of royal power in the Church, it was tragically real to him, and for some time he remained doubtful —a fact which partly explains his various recantations, which began with an attempt to acknowledge the Papacy only on the precise ground of royal command. It is an illustration of the difficulties with which the doctrine of the royal supremacy was to meet when royal policy did not coincide with that of those who had originally maintained the idea. This led to the change from the original Protestant high doctrine of the State to the Puritan echoing of the old Donatist, *Quid imperatori cum ecclesia?* which is first made explicit in Ponet's *Treatise of Politike Power*, written during the author's exile at this time.

Apart from the tale of continuing persecution, the **latter** part of Mary's reign offers little of significance in the story of the English Reformation. The administration became increasingly discredited and unpopular, as Mary's devotion to her husband, whose love for her was little more than conventional, led England into a war with France, despite all the provisions made at the time of the royal wedding that Philip's position in England should not automatically tie English policy to Spanish. It was a war from which the country gained nothing and suffered on the contrary the severe loss of Calais, last of the English Continental possessions, and for 200 years her stronghold on the other side of the Straits of Dover. The Spanish alliance too had the paradoxical result of embroiling the newly reconciled country with the Papacy, not for any fault of its own, but as the result of the election of a Pope, Paul IV, whose hatred of Spain amounted to mania. In May of 1557 he revoked the legatine commission of Cardinal Pole, and later summoned him to Rome to answer charges of heresy—the supposed prevalence of heresy in unlikely quarters being another topic upon which Paul IV held unbalanced ideas. This provoked from Mary the somewhat Henrician threat that if there were charges of this kind against her Cardinal 'she would, in observance of the laws and privileges of her realm, refer them to the cognizance and decision of her own ecclesiastical courts'. It is, indeed, interesting to speculate whether, if the Marian experiment had lasted longer, conflicts of the old type would have arisen between the English Crown and the Papacy, or perhaps between Church and State in England. For this had not been the only straw to show the possible direction of a future wind. We have already called attention to the restrictive provisions of the Act by which England resumed obedience to Rome, which ensured that the Pope did not gain by his restoration powers which he had not held before the breach. It was noteworthy, too, that Parliament offered considerable opposition to Mary's proposal to give up the Annates which Henry had appropriated to the Crown, as in conscience she felt bound to do. And it is intriguing to find that it was thought necessary for Pole to get royal permission for the exercise of his legatine powers in England, lest he should fall under the penalties of the Praemunire law which had destroyed Wolsey. The analogy of other Catholic powers in post-Reformation times suggests that, had the bonds with Rome not been broken again in 1558, collisions between Crown and Papacy and Erastian legislation might nevertheless have marked English history. Even with the bishops Henrician habits of thought died hard; it is amusing to find Bonner ending his official notification to his diocese of the reconciliation with Rome, which explains how individual laymen can obtain absolution for their share in the schism, with the words 'God save the kynge and the quene'.

But all this must remain in the fascinating but unprofitable realm of historical speculation. In fact Mary died, weary and despondent at the ill success of her work, in November 1558 and Pole within a day of her. And with them died the effort to which both had devoted all their energies, the restoration of the ancient English constitution of Church and State. The story of the English Reformation was far from complete; it was to go on until 1660 and beyond. But it would be with fresh problems and with different actors.

Epilogue

ALTHOUGH THIS BOOK does not deal with the later, and in a sense more formative, stages of the English Reformation —which, it is to be hoped, will be described in another volume of this series—yet something must be said of them in general, if our story is to be rounded off. For the long historical process known as the English Reformation did not end in 1558. In one sense it has not ended yet: for religious unity in this country was broken in the sixteenth century and has never since been restored. The history of the later sixteenth and earlier seventeenth centuries is that of the breakdown of the Tudor attempt to hold together a national Church, conterminous with the English nation. And, even within that Church, as it has survived the schisms from it which began in Elizabeth's reign, there has never been uniformity of opinion and only at times uniformity of practice; the Church of England is the only religious body in Europe in which the battle of Reformation and Counter-Reformation has never been fought to a finish and is still in progress. The accession of Elizabeth therefore, though a turning-point, is in no sense the terminus of the Reformation in England.

A turning-point however it was in the fullest sense. For in November 1558, when Mary died, there was no certainty about which way matters religious would turn. The new queen, though she had outwardly conformed under her sister's rule, was known not to share Mary's rigid Catholicism. She had been suspected of complicity in Wyatt's rebellion and kept under surveillance thereafter: whether or not she was privy to the plottings of the French party who opposed the Spanish influence, she was certainly the successor to the throne for whom they wished. Moreover, the reign of Mary had ended in disaster and the queen's religion was as unpopular as her policy, with which it was bound up. That policy had led to a war with France in the interests of Spain and so to the loss of Calais, England's last foothold on the Continent. At the same time the persecution, not merely of great men or intriguers, but of humble folk whose only offence was their interpretation of Christianity, had aroused the sympathy which suffering never fails to elicit from Englishmen, even when they do not wholly share the sufferer's viewpoint. The memories of Smithfield, fanned as they were later by Foxe's painstaking collection of the records of the Protestant martyrs, played a great part in the way things went in Elizabeth's first years and were to become a potent factor in English opinion right to the end of the period of religious strife and further. As we have seen, the reversal of Henry VIII's policy and the reunion with Rome had never been received so readily as the undoing of the Edwardine revolution, and the events which followed it did not make it more popular. In the last part of Mary's reign discontent was becoming more and more open. In December 1555 the bill by which Mary relinquished the Annates seized from the Pope by her father was passed by the Commons only after considerable pressure and by a majority of sixty-seven voices, with amendments which relieved the lay possessors of former church properties from any obligation to pay taxes to the Papacy. In 1556 plots and small risings took place and in 1557 Thomas Stafford, who had some hereditary pretensions to the throne, seized Scarborough Castle for a while. Even if Mary had lived longer her throne might not have been too secure, nor is it certain that she would in process of time have succeeded in maintaining her religious settlement.

But it was not equally obvious at first what would be the religious policy of the new regime. Elizabeth's personal religion is hard to estimate. She had been brought up partly under Protestant influences and she had an hereditary grievance against the Papacy which had condemned her mother's marriage and so made her a bastard. (But it must be remembered that Cranmer, at Henry VIII's behest, had done the same.) There are, however, signs that Elizabeth's sympathies were not with the extremer Protestants. She showed at least a sentimental attachment to Catholic ceremonial and the crucifix and candles in her private chapel were long a grievance to the iconoclastic feelings of many of her subjects; she had a strong prejudice against married clergy and there is every reason to believe that the efforts of the government to put down incipient Puritanism had her personal support and indeed her instigation. Yet she never listened very seriously to the overtures which came to her from Rome or the Catholic states of Europe and there is nothing to show that the revival of the Edwardine liturgy (with mitigations) was distasteful to her. She had indeed the English taste for eclecticism and a feminine disregard for complete consistency. It is probable too that she was not deeply religious by nature and viewed the controversies of the day with a certain detachment. Her court was never noticeable for piety; indeed a secularist type of Renaissance culture was more characteristic of it and at times religious scepticism and dabblings in astrology and magic were the fashion there. The queen too shared the general taste for spoliation of Church property and the undoing of Mary's attempts to reverse the alienations of Edwardine days and re-endow religion was among the very first measures of the new government.

In a sense, this relative indifference was the reason for the immunity of England from religious war such as was nearly to destroy France in the later sixteenth century and devastate Germany in the early seventeenth. The policy of the English administration never had the rigid logic of Continental Catholic or Protestant governments. It was slow to persecute actively and waited for signs of resistance before it resorted to force. It was as insistent as its predecessors upon religious conformity and it caused annoyance by its persistent imposition of the settlement upon which it eventually decided;

but it did not go looking for trouble and, even when it did come to hunting down opponents, its action was spasmodic and not always consistent. Elizabeth could protect Roman Catholic 'recusant' musicians even in her own Chapel Royal: Byrd remained its organist from 1570 to the end of the reign. Recusant peers were not excluded from the House of Lords. Puritanism survived government repression within the framework of the State Church to become a potent force in the next century. There was never a whole-hearted attempt to discover and root out utterly religious dissidence. It cannot with honesty be maintained, as Elizabeth's advisers liked to claim, that no one was persecuted by her for their religion, since the penal legislation against Roman Catholics specifically forbade practices which were a necessary part of their faith and demanded a conformity they could not in conscience yield. But it can be said that the excommunication of the queen by Pius V in 1570 and the claim to depose her contained in his bull, followed as it was by plots in favour of Mary Stuart as pretender to the throne and by warlike activity on the part of Spain, had most to do with the sharpening of the laws against recusancy.

At the beginning of the reign the lack of fanaticism shown by the new queen and her advisers made it even doubtful what line they would take. The Marian persecution was necessarily stopped at once and there were many indications that religious change from Marian orthodoxy was favoured by those in power, but the form that change would take was at least doubtful until a year had passed. The interesting memorandum called *A Device for the Alteration of Religion* (once believed to be the work of Cecil, who had become the chief adviser of Elizabeth, but, in the view of Sir John Neale, merely an anonymous example of several memoranda offering advice to the government) shows both the government's consciousness of its difficulties and its resolve to alter the existing system of religion. It suggests effecting changes at the first meeting of Parliament lest delay should weaken its position. It is aware of the danger which may come from French intervention on behalf of Mary Stuart and from

Scotland, and hopes to ward off both by diplomacy. It expects opposition from the Marian clergy of course, and from Mary's lay supporters—a body, however, of older men, who are to be supplanted in office by new and younger persons of a different outlook—and proposes to involve both in conflict with the law and reduce them to submission. In the period before Parliament meets a new liturgical programme is to be worked out by divines of Reforming sympathies, ready to be put into effect by legislation. At the same time the administration is conscious that danger will come also from the more zealous Protestants, who, in their exile abroad, had been showing dissatisfaction even with the second Edwardine Prayer Book. Some will 'call the alteration a cloaked papistry or a mingle-mangle'—a very accurate prophecy of the left-wing opposition which was to appear and grow steadily to the end of the reign.

In the event things fell out much as envisaged by this document, but not by Elizabeth's design. Her plan, it would seem, was for the time being to content herself with the restoration of the Royal Supremacy, without striking liturgical change in a Protestant direction except for the single step of restoring the chalice to communicants—a course which seemed wise before the balance of religious opinion in England could be weighed and at a time when foreign relations were in a dangerous condition, since part of the legacy of Mary was a war with France. The intransigence of a House of Commons dominated by Protestant feeling, spearheaded by a resolute handful of returned exiles, doomed this design to defeat, a fact which became obvious when Elizabeth's first Parliament met in January 1559. Presented with a Supremacy bill, the Commons tried to enlarge its scope to include the restoration of the Second Edwardine Prayer Book. The Lords, almost certainly acting under royal direction, rejected their amendments, but the lower House then made it clear that, however much they were opposed to papal authority, they would pass no Supremacy legislation unless there went with it measures to restore the Edwardine Reformation. Checked in this way, the Queen was about to dissolve Parliament and thus shelve for the time being the whole problem, when, with dramatic suddenness, she changed her mind, almost certainly upon receipt of the news that peace was about to be concluded with France, so that the external danger was alleviated. Parliament was merely adjourned over Easter and then, on its resumption, Elizabeth acceded to the wishes of the Commons, with the result that May found her giving the royal assent to both an Act of Supremacy and an accompanying Act of Uniformity. Both embodied modifications of their original aims. Reacting to scruples felt by some Protestants, as well as by Catholics, about the propriety of a woman's being described as Head of the Church, the Queen claimed merely the title of Supreme Governor—a distinction without practical difference in the powers it gave her. On the other hand she secured small but significant alterations in the text of the Second Edwardine Prayer Book restored by the Uniformity Act, which made it seem less blatantly Protestant. The Declaration on Kneeling, which had explicitly denied the Real Presence, was omitted. To the form of words used in administering the elements to the communicants, which made no reference to the inward part of the sacrament, were prefixed the corresponding formulae of 1549, which spoke of the Body and Blood of Christ. Thus the Elizabethan liturgy, although it did not require belief in a presence of Christ in the elements, equally did not deny one. From the Litany was removed the offensive reference to the Pope, which otherwise would have had to be heard by worshippers every Sunday. Finally, both the Act of Uniformity and the Prayer Book contained a provision which in theory (for in practice it was ignored from the beginning) retained in Anglican worship the traditional church ornaments and ministerial vestments of the Middle Ages ordered in the 1549 Book, but abolished from 1552 until Mary's accession.

Such is the curious origin of the phenomenon known as the Elizabethan Settlement of religion, reconstructed in its intricate parliamentary detail by the acute and convincing researches of Sir John Neale. The effects of the tussle in the first half of 1559 were to be far-reaching, for, despite the ingenious, if meagre, provisions she had obtained to try to reconcile conservative religious opinion to the liturgy, it was obvious that Elizabeth had been forced by her Protestant Commons to go further in reaction from Marian policy than she had intended, at least in the first year of her reign. To have her hand forced in this way was no doubt distasteful to one who shared to the full the Tudor dislike of contradiction from below, and the ill will she bore to the Puritan party all through her reign stemmed in all probability from her resentment. It remains however true that to this extent the Elizabethan Settlement was only to a limited degree genuinely Elizabethan, nor was it regarded by a good proportion of her subjects, Roman Catholic sympathizers on the one hand, and radical Protestants, who had already come to consider the Prayer Book of 1552 insufficiently Protestant, on the other, as a permanent settlement.

Protestant radicalism was further demonstrated in the first decade of the reign when a bitter 'Vestiarian' controversy, caused by the decision of the government to enforce at least a minimum of ceremony in the services of the Church, gave rise to embittered disputes and coercion of the recalcitrants by the authorities—a situation not made easier by the fact that most of the new bishops, upon whom Elizabeth had to rely to enforce her policy, were at least sympathetic to the attitude of those radicals who thought, as Cecil had foreseen, the new settlement a 'cloaked papistry'. Indeed, throughout the reign, the Elizabethan administration was in a position analogous to that of the sort of ministry in a modern parliamentary democracy which depends for its majority upon a group of parties of differing outlook, each of which, as the price of its support, demands concessions. Unless a return was to be made to Marian papistry—a solution to which, on both religious and political grounds, Cecil and his associates were opposed—some kind of accommodation must be made with those who thought that religious reform was only half accomplished, for there were not enough of the middle way to form a sufficiently strong *bloc* against Rome.

For, after the confusion of the first years, the Roman Catholics began increasingly to form an organized opposition. At first they had no clear programme, beyond doing their best to prevent the passing of the new religious legislation and avoiding conformity to it when once it was passed. The requirements of the oath of supremacy from the clergy soon deprived them of their natural leaders for, with one exception, the Marian bishops refused the oath and were deprived of their sees, most spending the rest of their lives in the custody of the government. Many parish priests—their number cannot be really ascertained and is still a matter of dispute—for the same reason were deprived of their livings. From these came the first of the clergy who secretly and illegally ministered to the spiritual needs of the recusants, though as time went on the Marian priests were first reinforced and finally superseded by the newly ordained exiles who were educated abroad, and then sent back to what the Papists were learning to call 'the English mission'. The 'seminary priest' was to the Elizabethan government both a more dangerous and a more reprehensible man than the Marian who declined conformity. Not only was he breaking national unity by seeking Orders elsewhere than from the official source—the national bishops—but he was doing so in the design of subverting the Queen's church discipline. Consequently the law marked him out for special penalties and the government pursuivants sought for him with special zeal.

It must always be remembered, in considering the whole period before 1660, that as yet the idea of differing religious denominations in one country was foreign and repulsive to the minds of contemporaries. The medieval idea of Church and State as two aspects of one community still held the field in all minds, with its corollary that dissent of any kind could not be tolerated. The Henrician changes in the relations of Church and State had indeed produced a stronger form of this conception, since as a result of them the State and not the Church was the dominant partner in the alliance and the sovereign had, both in theory and practice, the right to determine religion. As we have seen, the circumstances of

Mary's re-establishment of Catholicsm did little to modify this state of mind. Now however, once it became apparent that the settlement of 1559 could not easily be altered, two groups permanently opposed to the state religion came into more and more distinct existence. The Roman Catholics slowly ceased to think of the national Church as *their* Church temporarily captured by heretics and began instead to regard it as an heretical sect, which had been established by the government. Its ministrations must therefore be refused in favour of a counter-organization which they regarded as the true Church in England. This revision of outlook shows itself in the increasingly rigid refusal to attend Anglican services, from which the Popish 'recusants', as they were legally known, gained their name. At first it had been common for those who rejected the Elizabethan Establishment to attend its services at least occasionally to escape the fines which the law imposed upon non-churchgoers, supplementing this with illegal Masses and other services in private houses. The practice was soon regarded as raising an issue of conscience and Rome decided against its lawfulness, though the difficulty the papal missionaries found in getting this view accepted among the recusants shows how far the old idea still exercised a partly unconscious influence upon those who in their earlier lives had known one national organization of religion alone and could not easily conceive any other notion. But in time the new outlook prevailed and a clearer line began to appear between those who were merely dissatisfied with the new services and those who regarded them as the services of an apostate religious body. By the end of the reign partial or occasional conformity on the part of the Papists was regarded by their Church—now a rival organization in England—as unlawful. It continued on the part of those who refused to take the official condemnation seriously or sought to save their property and status in society by compromising their consciences, but it could never, as once seemed possible, become the basis of a religious peace. The conflict between the government and the recusants can better be understood when it is seen in this light:

it was a war between those who wished to base national spiritual unity upon one organization and those who wished to base it upon another and, as such, war to the knife.

It must be remembered, too, that in parts of the country—notably in the North—the Elizabethan settlement hardly existed before 1570 or later. The reports of the bishops show how powerless they were to make the Northerners (always conservative in religious matters) accept the new liturgy or, in some cases, even to secure its observance by the official clergy. The resistance of the North was partly broken by the defeat of the rising of the Northern Earls in support of Mary Queen of Scots in 1569. But it remained, to Elizabeth's death and far later, a centre of slowly decreasing recusancy and, indeed, still provides one of the chief centres of English Roman Catholicism. The concern of the government about recusancy and the perpetual fear among Protestants of a revival of Popery (which was one factor in the spread of Puritanism) can best be understood if we remember that Roman Catholicism, in the South largely an underground movement, was in other parts of the country a visible and strong opposition.

At the other pole, but hardly less opposed to official policy, stood Puritanism. The Puritans never developed the idea of themselves as a denomination to the same extent as the Papists; down to 1660 most conceived their mission to be a purification of the national Church, of which they hoped to seize control. Nor did they so much object to attending the legal services as to conforming to the details of the state liturgy. Their movement had begun with a refusal on the part of the Puritanical clergy to wear the surplice: it went on to other matters of conformity—the use of the ring in marriage, the right to offer extempore prayer, and so on. The Puritan laity supported the clergy who declined to conform and sometimes rejected the ministrations of those who did or who offended their sense of propriety in other ways. But they were essentially disgruntled members of the national Church—not seceders from it. Only in a very few cases in Elizabeth's reign did separatist movements of a Puritan type appear. The great mass of the Puritans wanted toleration for their views inside the Church and not outside—or, rather, they wished their views to be accepted and to prevail in the national establishment of religion. As time went on, however, the reforms they demanded became more radical: it was not just a few prayers or ceremonies they wanted to be altered, nor even a new liturgy for which they wished: the whole structure of the Church of England was to them defective, because so largely unaltered from the medieval pattern.

Thus the Puritans objected to episcopacy, partly because they drew their inspiration from Geneva, and believed the Calvinist system of ministry and church government there set up to be that which was demanded by the letter of Scripture. That system, which Scotland also adopted and which was indeed necessarily the norm wherever pure Calvinism gained the day, taught the parity of ministers, that is, the essential identity of the orders of bishops and presbyters, and made the chief authority in the Church assemblies called 'presbyteries', which consisted of a mixture of preaching elders (ministers) and lay elders chosen from the laity. It went with a rigid discipline over the lives of the faithful exercised by the presbyteries' use of the weapon of excommunication. This was the pattern after which the Puritans wanted the Church of England to be remodelled.

To understand its attractiveness to a large element of the more thoughtful members of the Elizabethan Church one must remember the disorder by which that Church was beset. The storms of the period since 1547 had worked havoc with church organization and in addition, whatever doctrinal and liturgical changes had been made, nothing which could seriously be called reform had been effected in the administrative sphere. The creaking, cumbrous, and sometimes corrupt machinery of the ecclesiastical courts still ground on its way as before and had not greatly changed since the Petition of the Commons had called attention to its abuses in 1532. The proposed revision of the Canon Law, provided for then by the Submission of the Clergy, had never taken place, though Cranmer had drawn up a proposed new code, the *Reformatio Legum Ecclesiasticarum.* The old evils of plurality, non-residence of pastors, and the like continued much as before, made if anything more inevitable in an impoverished Church. Indeed it has been said, without much exaggeration, that none of the characteristic medieval abuses in administration were reformed in England until Parliament took in hand the cleansing of the Church after the Reform Bill of 1832. To these old evils new ones were added by the spoliations of Edward's reign, which were repeated in Elizabeth's, and by the disputes and proscriptions between 1547 and 1559. There was a shortage of clergy, which the bishops attempted to provide for by appointing lay readers to perform services in the churches without ordained incumbents; they were often men of little education and sometimes of bad character. Livings were too impoverished to support their holders adequately and clerical poverty led to unclerical lives when men had somehow to supplement their regular income. The universities, which had been storm centres of the Reformation disputes, were disorganized by those quarrels and the expulsions they caused and were failing to produce a sufficient number of trained ordinands. Possibly never has the state of the Church of England in the parishes been so deplorable as in Elizabeth's time. Some idea of the condition into which the parochial system could get may be gathered, for example, from Mr. Douglas Price's researches into the records of the Diocese of Gloucester. Even as late as the early seventeenth century, though much had been done to improve matters, the picture given in the autobiography of Richard Baxter (born in 1615) of what his native part of Shropshire was like in his youth is striking:

We lived in a country that had but little preaching at all: in the village where I was born there were four readers successively in six years' time, ignorant men and two of them immoral in their lives; who were all my schoolmasters. In the village where my father lived, there was a reader of about eighty years of age that never preached, and had two churches about twenty miles distant: his eyesight failing him, he said Common Prayer without book:

but for the reading of the Psalms and Chapters, he got a common thresher and day labourer one year, and a tailor another year: (for the Clerk could not read well): and at last he had a kinsman of his own, (the excellentest stageplayer in all the country, and a good gamester and good fellow) that got Orders and supplied one of his places! . . . Within a few miles about us, were near a dozen more Ministers that were near eighty years old apiece, and never preached; poor ignorant readers, and most of them of scandalous lives: only three or four constant competent preachers lived near us, and these (though conformable all save one) were the common marks of the people's obloquy and reproach, and any that had but gone to hear them, when he had no preaching at home, was made the derision of the vulgar rabble, under the odious name of a *Puritane*.

Small wonder that a system so new and so tightly organized as that of Geneva made an appeal and that 'prophesyings', meetings of the clergy for mutual improvement, tended to convert themselves into the equivalents of Calvinistic presbyteries, taking little notice of episcopal authority or of the official Church organization and becoming laws to themselves. Even had there been no doctrinal urge towards it, Puritanism might well have been attractive to some for the mere sake of spiritual efficiency, especially as men found the Puritans always pleading for practical reform of abuses. They no doubt exaggerated the extent of the disorder so as to make their demands more plausible, and their characteristic temptation was priggishness; but the disorder was undeniable and the Puritans were in many respects the most vital spiritual force in the State Church when their movement began. Moreover their appeal lay to a higher authority than that of the State in matters of religion. Whether they understood it rightly or not, their standard in all things was the revealed Word of God in Scripture. To this extent at least, they, no less than the Papist recusants, represent a protest against state-given religion which could claim no higher sanction than the will of the sovereign.

However, their spiritual monopoly was not to last. The latter part of Elizabeth's reign saw the rise of a group of theologians who were to defend her settlement with other

weapons than the mere appeal to the *fait accompli*. Richard
Hooker, originally a protégé of Bishop Jewel (who in his
day had been the most effective defender of the Elizabethan
system against Rome), became Master of the Temple in 1584
and at once entered into controversy with Travers, the Puritan
Reader of the same London church. Out of the dispute
came eventually the *Ecclesiastical Polity*, the great work in
which the Elizabethan system was defended upon grounds of
philosophy and theology and the conception of a State
religion elevated from mere Erastianism to a restatement in
different terms of the old medieval notion of Church and
Nation as one community. Hooker was virtually the first
of a long line of Anglican divines who, with many differences in
detail of outlook, agreed in repudiating Puritan theology
and policy and continued to develop a tradition by which
the challenge of Puritanism was defeated and its adherents
driven from the Church of England after their temporary
triumph in the Civil War. At last a Church constitution which
had taken form largely as an expedient in the chaos of 1559
found a soul and voice of its own.

So, from the disputes of the period before 1558, there
eventually emerged three main currents of English religious
life. The history of what may be called the later period of
the English Reformation is that of their definition and struggle
for supremacy.

Roman Catholicism formed itself into a Church which
had finally rejected the whole conception of the Protestant
Reformation. Its adherents were in touch with the reformed
Catholicism of the Continent, whence they drew their priesthood and their educational and devotional resources. A
minority movement, it was nevertheless a vigorous one and
survived by the heroism with which it faced spasmodic
bloody persecution and permanent ostracism and repression.
At times it seemed, through the influence of political events,
to have chances of returning to power, and it was not clear
until 1688, when the experiment of a Roman Catholic King of
England ended in revolution, that it had lost all chance of
doing so and must for the future resign itself at best to a

tolerated and competitive position in the life of the nation.

On the other wing, Puritanism represented the desire to assimilate the English Church in all respects to the straitest form of Continental Protestantism, namely the Calvinist theology and discipline. It possessed strength and vitality, though its supporters were usually the less characteristic members of English society, enthusiasts and propagandists who came mostly from the developing middle class of merchants, successful artisans, and the newer landlords. It was able to maintain itself as a permanent opposition to official policy all through the reigns of Elizabeth, James I, and Charles I, until, as the spiritual mainspring of the revolution inspired by religious, political, and economic grievances against the Crown, it defeated and destroyed the king in the Civil War. Then, in the hour of its triumph, it split into factions and was forced to acquiesce in the return of the Anglican system together with the monarchy in 1660, when Puritanism was expelled from the national Church and had to organize itself in a series of dissident Nonconformist churches.

Finally there was the almost indefinable and yet increasingly real central force of Anglicanism, as we are forced to call it for want of a better name. This represented those who declined to follow Rome and yet rejected decisively the supposed logical alternative of Geneva. This attitude was characteristic of one aspect of the English temperament in that it was slow to define itself and never did so completely. Even when it grew into a theology it remained a mood more than a system. Indeed, it contained within itself potentialities of more than one kind, which made it, even when separated out from Roman Catholicism and Puritanism, still capable of division. Those potentialities were to develop in time into both eighteenth-century Methodism and Evangelicalism on the one hand and ninteenth-century Anglo-Catholicism on the other, and Methodism was to cause yet another schism in English religion. It is perhaps wrong to describe the central stream resulting from the floods of the sixteenth century by any such definite name as Anglicanism, for it was never a movement nor a cohesive party. According to one's predilections one may regard it as an undifferentiated residuum left by the disintegrating forces of the Reformation acting upon medieval Christianity, as a new *tertium quid* between Catholicism and Protestantism, as a new form of Catholicism, or as a survival of something earlier than the medieval situation out of which the Reformation grew. It may indeed have something of all these things in it; in any case we have not yet seen the end of the story. The final proof that one is right in recognizing an element of uniqueness in the English Reformation, when one compares it with its Continental analogues, is that its results have been nowhere in Christendom precisely paralleled. England is the land of exception—in her religious as much as in her constitutional development.

Select Bibliography

The following list, which does not aim at any degree of completeness, may serve to indicate, to those who wish to follow up in greater detail the story of the English Reformation before 1558, some of the chief sources and modern studies which will be of most use to them.

1. BIBLIOGRAPHY

READ, CONYERS (ed.): *Bibliography of British History; Tudor Period, 1485–1603.* (2nd ed. Oxford, 1959.)

Invaluable for books published up to its date of publication. Produced by a team of scholars under the auspices of the American Historical Association and the Royal Historical Society of Great Britain. Annotated and indexed.

2. COLLECTIONS OF DOCUMENTS

BREWER, J. S., and GAIRDNER, JAMES: *Letters and Papers, Foreign and Domestic, of the Reign of Henry VIII.* (21 vols. in 33 parts. London, 1862–1910. A new and fuller edition by R. H. Brodie was begun in 1920.)

The fullest collection of all state and other papers of the period.

CARDWELL, EDWARD: *Synodalia*, Vol. I. (Oxford, 1842.)

Contains some of the acts of Convocation from 1547 onwards.

—: *Documentary Annals of the Reformed Church of England*, Vol. I. (Oxford, 1839.)

Useful collection of official documents.

EHSES, STEFAN: *Römische Dokumente zur Geschichte der Ehescheidung Heinrichs VIII von England 1527–1534.* (Görres Gesellschaft, Paderborn, 1893.)

Documents on the divorce not in Pocock. Results summarized by James Gairdner in *The English Historical Review*, xi and xii, 1896–7.

ELTON, G. R.: *The Tudor Constitution: Documents and Commentary.* (Cambridge, 1960.)

FOXE, JOHN: *Actes and Monuments.* Popularly known as *The Book of Martyrs.* A partisan hagiographical work on the Protestant side, but valuable for documents used. Has never been satisfactorily edited; latest full edition by Josiah Pratt, 8 vols., in 1877. See *Dictionary of National Biography*, art. Foxe, for details of editions and criticisms of them. Also J. F. MOZLEY: *John Foxe and his Book.* (London, 1940.)

GEE, H., and HARDY, W. J.: *Documents illustrative of English Church History.* (London, 1896. Frequently reprinted.)
Contains most of the important Acts of Parliament.

HUGHES, PAUL L., and LARKIN, JAMES F. (ed.): *Tudor Royal Proclamations*, Vol. I: *The Early Tudors (1485–1553).* (New Haven and London, 1964.)

POCOCK, NICHOLAS: *Records of the Reformation.* (2 vols. Oxford, 1870.)
Documents on Henry VIII's divorce.

STRYPE, JOHN: *Ecclesiastical Memorials.* (3 vols. in ed. of Strype's *Works.* Oxford, 1820–40.)
Documents from Henry VIII to Mary.

—: *Memorials of Archbishop Cranmer.* (3 vols. Oxford, 1848–54.)
Documents relating to Cranmer.

TANNER, J. R.: *Tudor Constitutional Documents, 1485–1603.* (Cambridge, 1922.)

THURSTON, HERBERT: 'The canon law of the divorce' in *The English Historical Review*, xix (1904), 632–645.

TYTLER, P. F.: *England under the Reigns of Edward VI and Mary.* (2 vols. London, 1839.)
Interesting collection of documents.

WILKINS, DAVID: *Concilia Magnae Britanniae et Hiberniae.* (4 vols. London, 1737.)
Prints records of Convocation not destroyed in the Fire of London in 1666, but not always completely or accurately.

3. OTHER SOURCES

The works of the principal English Reformers were edited by the Parker Society (56 vols.) at Cambridge in the middle of the nineteenth century. This series contains the valuable *Epistolae Tigurinae* (1848), translated as *Original Letters relative to the English Reformation, 1531–1558.* (2 vols. 1846–7.)

Many of the important chronicles will be found in the Camden Society collections. (London, 1838 onwards.)

CAMPBELL, W. E. (ed.): *Sir Thomas More: The Dialogue against Tyndale.* (London, 1927.)

HALL, EDWARD: *Chronicle.* Ed. Charles Whibley. (2 vols. London, 1904.)
Important for reign of Henry VIII.

JANELLE, PIERRE: *Obedience in Church and State: Three Political Tracts by Stephen Gardiner.* (Cambridge, 1930.)

MULLER, J. A.: *The Letters of Stephen Gardiner.* (Cambridge, 1933.)

NICHOLS, J. G.: *Literary Remains of King Edward VI.* (2 vols. Roxburghe Club, London, 1857.)

RASTELL, W. (ed.): *The Workes of Sir Thomas More.* (London, 1557.)

4. OLD NARRATIVES

BURNET, GILBERT: *History of the Reformation of the Church of England.* (London, 1679–1715. Ed. Nicholas Pocock, 7 vols., Oxford, 1865.)
Contains documents.

COLLIER, JEREMY: *An Ecclesiastical History of Great Britain.* (London, 1708–14. Ed. Thomas Lathbury, 9 vols., London, 1852.)

FULLER, THOMAS: *Church History of Britain.* (London, 1655. Ed. J. S. Brewer, 6 vols., Oxford, 1845.)

HEYLYN, PETER: *Ecclesia Restaurata.* (London, 1661. Ed. J. C. Robertson, Cambridge, 1849.)
Attacked Fuller from High Church angle.

SANDERS, NICHOLAS: *De origine ac progressu schismatis Anglicani liber.* (Cologne, 1585.) Eng. tr. ed. D. Lewis (London, 1877).
Roman Catholic almost contemporary account.

These old works are often of value, as sometimes based upon material not now extant.

5. LATER NARRATIVES

CONSTANT, G.: *La Réforme en Angleterre: I. Le schisme anglican: Henri VIII.* (Paris, 1930.) (Eng. tr. R. E. Scantlebury, *The Reformation in England; Henry VIII*, London, 1934.)

—: *La Réforme en Angleterre: II. Edouard VI.* (Paris, 1939.) (Eng. tr. E. I. Watkin, *The Reformation in England; Edward VI*, London, 1941.)
Both English translations omit some notes.

DICKENS, A. G.: *The English Reformation.* (London, 1964; new ed. 1966.)
The latest and most balanced full survey.

DIXON, R. W.: *History of the Church of England from the Abolition of the Roman Jurisdiction.* (6 vols., Oxford, 1878–1902.)
High Church standpoint.

FROUDE, J. A.: *History of England from the Fall of Wolsey to the Defeat of the Spanish Armada.* (12 vols., London, 1856–70; revised ed. 1862–70. Others later.)
Strongly anti-Catholic, not always accurate, but valuable.

GAIRDNER, JAMES: *Lollardy and the Reformation in England.* (4 vols., London, 1908–13.)

—: *The English Church in the Sixteenth Century from the Accession of Henry VIII to the Death of Mary.* (London, 1902.) (Vol. IV of *A History of the English Church*, ed. W. Hunt and W. R. W. Stephens.)
Both marked by a strong dislike of 'heretics'.

HUGHES, PHILIP: *The Reformation in England.* 3 vols. (London, 1950, 1953, and 1954.)
An unprejudiced and well-documented Roman Catholic account.

—: *Rome and the Counter-Reformation in England.* (London, 1942.)
Roman Catholic.

LINGARD, JOHN: *A History of England.* (8 vols., London, 1819–30. Enlarged ed., 10 vols., London, 1849—last revised by author. Later posthumous editions.)
A Roman Catholic pioneer in the use of documents.

NEALE, J. E.: *Elizabeth I and Her Parliaments: 1559–1581.* (London, 1953.)
Important new interpretation of the Elizabethan Settlement.

POWICKE, F. M.: *The Reformation of England.* (London, 1941.)
An interesting and well-balanced survey.

6. BIOGRAPHIES

CHAMBERS, R. W.: *Thomas More.* (London, 1935.)

DICKENS, A. G.: *Thomas Cromwell and the English Reformation.* (London, 1959.)

DUFFIELD, G. E. (ed.): *The Works of Thomas Cranmer.* Introd. by J. I. Packer. (Appleford, Berks., 1964.)

FRIEDMANN, PAUL: *Anne Boleyn: a Chapter of English History.* (2 vols., London, 1884.)

MATTINGLY, GARRETT: *Catherine of Aragon.* (London, 1942.)
New material from foreign archives.

MERRIMAN, R. B.: *The Life and Letters of Thomas Cromwell.* (2 vols., Oxford, 1902.)
Prints all Cromwell's letters.

MOZLEY, J. F.: *William Tyndale.* (London, 1937.)

MULLER, J. A.: *Stephen Gardiner and the Tudor Reaction.* (New York and London, 1926.)

POLLARD, A. F.: *Wolsey.* (London, 1929. New ed. Fontana Library, London, 1965, with Introd. by G. R. Elton.)

—: *England under Protector Somerset.* (London, 1900.)

PRESCOTT, H. F. M.: *Mary Tudor.* (London, 1952.)

RIDLEY, JASPER: *Thomas Cranmer.* (Oxford, 1962.)

SEEBOHM, FREDERIC: *The Oxford Reformers.* (3rd ed., London, 1887. Reprinted in Everyman's Library.)

STURGE, CHARLES: *Cuthbert Tunstal.* (London, 1938.)

7. BOOKS ON PARTICULAR SUBJECTS

BASKERVILLE, GEOFFREY: *English Monks and the Suppression of the Monasteries.* (London, 1937.)

CHAPMAN, HESTER D.: *The Last Tudor King: a Study of Edward VI.* (London, 1958.)

DICKENS, A. G.: *Lollards and Protestants in the Diocese of York: 1509–1558.* (London, 1959.)

DIETZ, F. C.: *English Government Finance, 1485–1558.* (Illinois University Studies in the Social Sciences, 9, iii, Urbana, Ill., U.S.A., 1920–21. Rep., London, 1964.)

DODDS, M. H. and RUTH: *The Pilgrimage of Grace.* (2 vols., Cambridge, 1915.)

GARRETT, C. H.: *The Marian Exiles, 1553–1559.* (Cambridge, 1938.)

GASQUET, F. A.: *Henry VIII and the English Monasteries.* (2 vols., London, 1888–89. Last ed. 1906.)

For criticism, see G. G. COULTON, *Medieval Studies.* (London, 1930.)

GASQUET, F. A., and BISHOP, EDMUND: *Edward VI and the Book of Common Prayer.* (London, 2nd ed. 1891.)

HOPF, C.: *Martin Bucer and the English Reformation.* (Oxford, 1946.)

JANELLE, PIERRE: *L'Angleterre catholique à la veille du schisme.* (Paris, 1935.)

KNOWLES, DOM DAVID: *The Religious Orders in England.* Vol. III: *The Tudor Age.* (Cambridge, 1959.)

A fully up to date and definitive account of the Dissolution.

MCGONILA, JAMES KELSEY: *English Humanists and Reformation Politics under Henry VIII and Edward VI.* (Oxford, 1965.)

MORISON, S.: *English Prayer Books.* (3rd ed., Cambridge, 1949.)

PORTER, H. C.: *Reformation and Reaction in Tudor Cambridge.* (Cambridge, 1958.)

PROCTER, F., and FRERE, W. H.: *A New History of the Book of Common Prayer.* (London, 1901, new ed. 1914. Often reprinted.)

RATCLIFF, EDWARD C.: *The booke of common prayer of the Churche of England: its making and revisions.* (London, 1949.)

ROSE-TROUP, FRANCES: *The Western Rebellion of 1549*. (London, 1913.)

RUPP, E. G.: *Studies in the Making of the English Protestant Tradition.* (Cambridge, 1947.)

SAVINE, A.: 'English Monasteries on the Eve of the Dissolution' in *Oxford Studies in Social and Legal History*, Vol. I. (Oxford, 1909.)

SCARISBRICK, J.: 'The Pardon of the Clergy, 1531' in *The Cambridge Historical Journal*, xii (1956), 22–39.

SMITH, H. MAYNARD: *Pre-Reformation England.* (London, 1938.)

—: *Henry VIII and the Reformation.* (London, 1948.)

SMITH, L. B.: *Tudor Prelates and Politics: 1536–1558.* (Princeton, N.J., 1953.)

THOMSON, JOHN A. F.: *The Later Lollards, 1414–1520.* (London, 1965.)

ZEEVELD, W. GORDON: *Foundations of Tudor Policy.* (Cambridge, Mass., 1948.)

Index